Text by Andrew Forbes and Ron Emmons
Editor: Jeffery Pike
Principal photography: David Henley/CPA
Cover photograph: Getty images/Glen Allison
Layout Concept: Klaus Geisler
Managing Editor: Tony Halliday

Berlitz POCKET GUIDE
Vietnam

First Edition 2004

PHOTOGRAPHY BY
David Henley/CPA, pages 10, 12, 15, 16, 18, 19, 21, 24, 26, 28, 29, 31, 32, 33, 35, 36, 37, 38, 39, 40, 45, 46, 47, 49, 50, 51, 52, 54, 55, 56, 58, 59, 60–1, 62, 64, 66, 67, 68, 70, 71, 73, 74, 77, 78, 80–1, 83, 86, 88, 90, 91, 93, 94, 96, 98, 101, 102, 103, 104, 106, 108; Jim Holmes, pages 3, 6, 9, 13, 43, 57, 85

CONTACTING THE EDITORS
Every effort has been made to provide accurate information in this publication, but changes are inevitable. The publisher cannot be responsible for any resulting loss, inconvenience or injury. We would appreciate it if readers would call our attention to any errors or outdated information by contacting Berlitz Publishing, PO Box 7910, London SE1 1WE, England.
Fax: (44) 20 7403 0290;
e-mail: berlitz@apaguide.co.uk
www.berlitzpublishing.com

Printed in Singapore by Insight Print Services (Pte) Ltd, 38 Joo Koon Road, Singapore 628990.
Tel: (65) 6865-1600. Fax: (65) 6861-6438

The mausoleum of Emperor Minh Mang is just one of several grand imperial tombs near the former capital, Hue (see page 53)

Chinese merchants built ornate assembly halls in the ancient city of Hoi An (see page 59)

Thousands of craggy islands make a boat excursion on Halong Bay a truly memorable experience (see page 43)

TOP TEN ATTRACTIONS

French colonial architecture gives central Saigon a distinguished air (see page 72)

The most striking and puzzling Cham monuments are the famous brick towers (see page 65)

The Great Cao Dai Temple in Tay Ninh is headquarters of an idiosyncratic religion (see page 81)

Hanoi's bustling and picturesque Old Quarter dates back to the 13th century (see page 28)

The claustrophobic tunnels of Cu Chi are a reminder of war (see page 77)

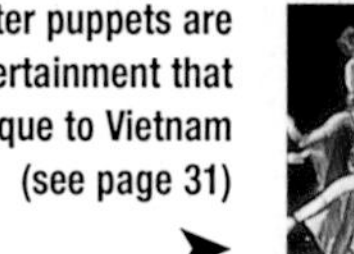

In the colourful hill town of Sa Pa (see page 45)

Water puppets are an entertainment that is unique to Vietnam (see page 31)

CONTENTS

A ➤ in the text denotes a highly recommended sight

Fact Sheets

VIETNAM AND ITS PEOPLE

For over 2,000 years Vietnam's development as a nation has been marked by the proximity of China. No country in Southeast Asia is culturally closer to China than Vietnam, and no other country in the region has spent so long fighting off Chinese domination – often at a terrible cost in lives, economic development and political compromise.

Perhaps because of the long years of rivalry, Vietnam has developed a powerful sense of national identity, placing the Viets somewhere between China and the rest of Southeast Asia, possessing a unique cultural heritage that is both strongly Sinicised and also distinctively Southeast Asian.

The Vietnamese have a modern slogan: *Vietnam is a country, not a war*. But for 30 years after World War II, Vietnam was almost synonymous with war, first with the French and later with the Americans. Vestiges of war remain in the bomb craters, abandoned military hardware and labyrinths of tunnels where entire villages endured the fighting. Today the craters have been converted into fishponds, the tunnels turned into a tourist attraction.

Looking westwards to their near neighbours in Thailand, the Vietnamese see the benefits that international tourism can bring (notably hard currency from abroad) but they also worry about the associated problems – loose morals, drugs, antisocial behaviour, Aids and, underlying it all, the threat of open debate, a free press and genuine opposition.

Still, in the 10 years since Vietnam first began to open up to the outside world, great changes have been made. Standards of accommodation have risen, thousands of new restaurants have opened, communications have improved

The Hoang Son mountains loom over the Yen River, southwest of Hanoi

and most of the country is now accessible. Still more importantly, as the regime has relaxed so have the Vietnamese people. Once characterised by a certain shyness or insecurity which sometimes manifested itself in a cool or reserved manner, the Vietnamese are now increasingly open, friendly and eager to meet foreign travellers.

The Country and its Climate

The Socialist Republic of Vietnam encompasses 329,566 sq km (127,245 sq miles) – slightly larger than the United Kingdom and Ireland added together. The country is long – over 1,600km (1,000 miles) from north to south – and narrow, being as little as 50km (32 miles) wide in the centre. The northernmost point lies just below the Tropic of Cancer, its southern extreme just above latitude 8°N, placing it squarely in the tropics. It shares land borders with China to the north and Laos and Cambodia to the west. In addition, Vietnam has a 3,450-km (2,156-mile) coastline along the South China Sea in the east. The capital, Hanoi, is located in the heart of the Red River Valley, in the north of the country. The largest city – called Saigon until 1975, and now Ho Chi Minh City – dominates the fertile Mekong Delta in the south.

Vietnam's long, narrow shape and location in the Southeast Asian monsoon zone gives rise to a complex climate that varies considerably from north to south. In the north, the winter from November to April is relatively cold and humid, and temperatures may fall as low as freezing point in the mountains around Sapa. Summer, between May and October, brings higher temperatures, heavy rain and sometimes typhoons. Both the north and centre experience their hottest months during June, July and August.

Southern Vietnam's climate is more Southeast Asian, with a relatively dry season from November to February, a hot season from February to April, when temperatures may reach 35°C (95°F), and heavy rains between May and October. During this period humidity rises to between 80 and 100 percent, and conditions can be sticky and uncomfortable.

Population and Language

About 90 percent of the people are ethnic Viets, also known as Kinh. They are probably descended from a number of diverse ethnic groups, the most important elements among which are Sinitic and Malayo-Polynesian. The remaining 10 percent of the population are divided among numerous ethnic groups.

Vietnam's 1 million Chinese constitute the most important ethnic minority. Nearly all are Hoa, or Chinese who are naturalised Vietnamese citizens. They live mostly in the south, in Ho Chi Minh City (especially Cholon) and in the Mekong Delta. The ancestors of the Hoa came principally from the southern Chinese provinces of Guangxi,

The rainy season in Ho Chi Minh City

Guangdong, Fujian, Zhejiang and Taiwan.

Cholon's Cantonese community worship at Thien Hau Pagoda

The Khmer, numbering around 500,000 and living mainly in the Mekong Delta, are ethnically identical to the Khmers of Cambodia and practise Theravada Buddhism. Ethnic minorities in the mountains of central and southern Vietnam form another significant group. Called *Montagnards* by the French, they include Muong, Ra De, Jarai, Banhar and Sedang living in the Central Highlands. Numbering around 750,000, they have long resisted Viet influence and remain culturally distinct to the present day.

The Chams inhabit the Phan Rang and Phan Thiet regions, as well as parts of the Mekong Delta. Once masters of the central coast, they now number fewer than 150,000. The coastal Cham are predominantly Hindu, while those of the Mekong Delta are Muslim. The highlands of the north are home to numerous other minorities. These include the Tay, of which there are just over a million. Other important highland groups in this region include the Tai (close relations to the various Tai-speaking groups of Laos, Thailand and China's Yunnan Province), the Hmong and the Nung.

The national language is Vietnamese, a complex fusion of Mon-Khmer, Tai and Chinese elements. It's not an easy language for the visitor to learn, though it is easy (and sensible) to acquire some elementary vocabulary to cover basic courtesies as well as food and travel-related terms. Fortunately, the script is Romanised, so placenames and menus are more readily decipherable than in neighbouring Laos and Cambodia. English is becoming widespread, especially among the young, while older people often still retain French as a second language.

Religion and Culture

Most Vietnamese consider themselves Buddhists, but are followers of the Mahayana doctrine, as taught in China, rather than the Theravada Buddhism of nearby Thailand, Laos and Cambodia. Traditional Vietnamese values respect and closely adhere to the teachings of Confucius, while many Viets are also influenced by Taoism. Yet they believe in locality spirits too, and practise a distinctly Southeast Asian form of spirit worship.

Vietnam's unique and complex cultural identity is in some ways paralleled by the geography of the country. The closer to China, the more Sinicised the land and its people seem. Conversely, in the centre and especially the south there is a much more Southeast Asian feel. This is apparent, to some degree, in the country's historical monuments. Hanoi is without doubt the country's major historic destination and owes much to Chinese culture and influence – its very name is derived from the Chinese *he nei*, or 'within the waters'. Traditional Vietnamese cul-

Thanks largely to the efforts of Jesuit missionaries and the country's long association with France, Vietnam has an estimated 8 million Christians (after the Philippines, the largest number in Southeast Asia), mostly Catholics and mostly found in the south of the country.

A bullock cart on the road from Hue to Danang

ture, such as water puppetry, music and dance, is best viewed in the Red River Delta, the ancestral homeland of the Viet people.

Further south the former Imperial City of Hue also owes a lot to Chinese cultural influences. Here, the Nguyen emperors conscientiously built their Forbidden City on the model of Beijing (albeit within a massive citadel based on the designs of the French military architect Sebastien de Vauban). Imperial ceremonies, too, were closely derived from those performed by the Chinese Emperor.

But beyond the Hai Van Pass, which divides the country south of Hue, things begin to change. This was formerly the territory of the Hinduised Kingdom of Champa, and all the way from My Son to Phan Thiet the country is studded with ancient brick towers honouring Vishnu, Shiva and other Hindu gods. There still remains a different, Southeast Asian flavour to this region which extends all the way to the Mekong Delta – home to the country's half-million ethnic Khmers. Not that Chinese influences are absent from the south: from the ancient port city of Hoi An to the teeming streets of Cholon, the culture of China has left its mark.

Landscape and Wildlife

Vietnam has more than its share of natural wonders, too. Halong Bay in the north rivals Thailand's Phang Nga Bay in the profusion of its extraordinary limestone islands and outcrops. The long central coast is dotted with fine beaches, notably at Loc Vinh, Nha Trang and Mui Ne. Here the visitor will find all kinds of watersports and some of the best seafood in the world.

The interior is dominated by the all-but-impenetrable mountains of the Annamite Cordillera and, further south, the Central Highlands. Vietnam is regarded as one of Asia's most biologically diverse countries – an evolutionary hotspot. The Vu Quang wildlife reserve has even been described as 'the Galapagos of Southeast Asia', with various previously unknown flora and fauna still being discovered.

The Vietnamese government has set up various National Parks as well as marine conservation sites. Two such jewels are the Bach Ma National Park in the Central Highlands, and Cat Tien National Park in the south. Bach Ma's inhabitants include the elusive clouded leopard. Cat Tien is one of only two places in the world where Javan rhinos are known to survive in the wild. In the early 1990s the Vietnamese government, with the help of the World Wildlife Fund (WWF), began turning its attention to the protection of marine areas, leading to the establishment of the Hon Mun Marine Park in Nha Trang. The park is now one of Vietnam's foremost snorkelling and scuba diving sites.

Lake fishing in Son La province

A BRIEF HISTORY

The early history of Vietnam, like that of all ancient countries, is lost in the mists of time and legend. What is clear beyond doubt is that the ancestors of today's Kinh (as the Vietnamese call themselves) first flourished three to four millennia ago in the fertile floodplains of southernmost China and the Red River Valley of Tonkin. The story of Vietnamese survival and their long fight for freedom and independence is one of southern territorial expansion – defending against China in the north, while systematically extending their power over the declining kingdoms of Champa and Cambodia to the south.

Legendary Kings

Vietnamese legend has it that King De Minh, descendant of a divine Chinese ruler, married an immortal mountain fairy. The product of their union, Kinh Duong, in turn married the daughter of the Dragon Lord of the Sea. Their son, Lac Long Quan or 'Dragon Lord of Lac', is considered the first Vietnamese king. To maintain peace with their powerful neighbours, the Chinese – a theme constant throughout Viet history – Lac Long Quan married Au Co, yet another Chinese immortal, who bore him 100 sons. Subsequently Lac Long Quan's eldest son succeeded him as the first king of the Hung Dynasty.

According to oral tradition, the Hung Dynasty had 18 kings, each of whom ruled for 150 years. This belief alone makes any attempt at accurately dating or even verifying these events quite pointless.

Rather than viewing the Hung Dynasty as a historical fact, it should be seen as a heroic legend set in mythical terms to glorify the early establishment of the Vietnamese nation. During this time the southward territorial imperative of both the Han Chinese and the Vietnamese was established, and thereby a rivalry that has lasted for millennia.

In 258BC Thuc Pan, ruler of Au Viet, overthrew the 18th Hung king and established a new Vietnamese state called Au Lac, with its capital at Co Loa just north of present-day Hanoi. Within half a century, in 207BC, a renegade Chinese general, Trieu Da, conquered Au Lac and established power over Nam Viet, a state based in what is now Guangxi in southern China and the Red River Delta of northern Vietnam. Chinese dominion over Nam Viet was confirmed in 111BC when the heirs of Trieu Da formally submitted to the Han emperor Wu Ti, establishing Chinese rule as far south as the Hai Van Pass and making Nam Viet the Chinese province of Giao Chau.

The Tran Quoc Pagoda in Hanoi dates from the Early Ly Dynasty

A Thousand Years of Chinese Rule

During the 1st century Chinese attempts to Sinicise the people of Giao Chau were partly successful but provoked widespread hostility among the Vietnamese. In AD40 this resulted in the first major Viet rebellion against the Chinese, led by the Trung sisters, two Viet ladies of noble birth who pro-

Hindu culture: a Cham carving of Shiva from My Son

claimed themselves joint queens of an independent Vietnam. The Trung sisters are still honoured as national heroines, but their attempt at breaking away from Chinese rule did not last. Just three years later, General Ma Vien re-established Chinese control over the territory and intensified the process of Sinification. The Vietnamese increasingly came under the Chinese spell, imitating the customs of the great northern neighbour they resented so much.

For the next nine centuries the Viets remained in thrall to the Chinese, despite a series of major rebellions. In 544 the Viet nationalist Ly Bon led a rising which achieved partial independence under the Early Ly Dynasty, but this was crushed by Chinese armies in 603. The victorious Chinese renamed the country An Nam, or 'Pacified South' – though this would prove to be wishful thinking. In 938 the Viet patriot Ngo Quyen decisively defeated the Chinese at the Battle of the Bach Dang River and reasserted Vietnamese independence after almost 1,000 years of Chinese domination. At last the Viets were free, but by this time they had become the most Sinicised people in Southeast Asia, in marked contrast to their Cham, Tai and Khmer neighbours, all of whom had fallen under the philosophic and religious influence of India.

The Vietnamese had learned at least one valuable lesson from their centuries of confrontation with China. The

Chinese threat wasn't going to go away, and they had to live with their northern neighbours. They achieved this by combining fierce resistance to Chinese aggression with contrite, even humble apologies to the Dragon Throne every time the Chinese were repelled. This rather clever system was formalised in 968 when King Dinh Tien, founder of the Dinh Dynasty, reaffirmed Vietnamese independence but agreed to pay tribute to the Chinese every three years. In a word, it was a matter of face.

Vietnam Moves South

From the 11th century on, Vietnam found new ways of imitating China, the neighbour it had learned both to admire and fear. Firstly, Buddhism began to make headway as a major religion in Vietnam – though this was the Mahayana faith introduced from China, and not the Theravada system practised elsewhere in Southeast Asia. Confucianism, too, was enthusiastically adopted from the Chinese and established as the basis of state administration.

Secondly, the Vietnamese people, hemmed in by the more populous Chinese to the north and the jagged mountains of the Annamite Cordillera to the west, began to expand in the only direction open to them – southwards. From their new capital at Thanh Long, or 'Ascending Dragon' (later renamed Hanoi) the long subjugation and conquest of the ancient Hindu Kingdom of Champa was begun.

Hanoi has at least 120 street names that commemorate struggles against foreign aggression. The list includes 58 celebrating victories over Chinese imperialism, 61 marking victories over French colonialism, but just two celebrating the defeat of the USA during the Second Indochina War.

The Viets continued to hold the north with consid-

Hien Nhon Gate to the Citadel at Hue, the Nguyen Lords' capital

erable success, defeating a Mongol invasion in 1279 at the Second Battle of the Bach Dang River. By the 14th century central Vietnam as far as the Hai Van Pass had been secured, with the city of Hue passing under Viet suzerainty. In 1428 yet another Chinese invasion was defeated by the national hero Le Loi. Meanwhile, to the south, Qui Nhon was seized from Champa in 1471, and the Cham Kingdom was reduced to a near-powerless rump.

So by the beginning of the 16th century everything seemed to be going well for Dai Viet, the Kingdom of the Vietnamese. But new troubles were just around the corner. In 1516 the first Westerners, in the form of Portuguese seafarers, arrived in the country. Moreover, in the distant south, as Champa crumbled, rival claimants to Hanoi's rule were emerging among the Viets themselves. In 1527 the country split in two, with the Mac (and subsequently Trinh) Lords ruling the Red River Delta region from

Hanoi, while the Nguyen Lords dominated the south of the country from their capital at Hue.

By the 17th century the French had replaced the Portuguese as the predominant Westerners in Vietnam, where they paid particular attention to the centre and the south. The French introduced Catholicism, which gradually spread throughout the country, despite the best efforts of the Confucian and Buddhist establishments. As a consequence, Vietnam was to become the second most Christian country in Asia, surpassed only by the Philippines. As a corollary of this missionary effort, the French priest Alexandre de Rhodes developed the Quoc Ngu system of Romanised Vietnamese script which is still used throughout the country today.

By 1757 Vietnam settlers had bypassed the tiny surviving rump of Champa near Phan Thiet and had begun their conquest of the Mekong Delta, until this time under Cambodian control. The Khmer settlement of Prey Nokor was taken from the Cambodians and renamed Saigon. Finally, in the 19th century, the last vestiges of Champa were snuffed out and Vietnam assumed full control over the territories which it controls today.

The Nguyen Emperors and French Conquest

In 1802 the Lord Nguyen Anh defeated his northern rivals and established the Nguyen Dynasty (1802–1945) at Hue, where he proclaimed himself Emperor Gia Long. For the first time in Vietnam's history, power

Imperial costumes from the tomb of Emperor Minh Hang (1820–41)

shifted south from the Red River Delta to the centre of the country. Yet the authority of the Nguyen did not remain unchallenged for long. In 1858 France seized both Danang and Saigon, laying the foundations for its colonies in Annam and Cochinchina. By 1883, supported by modern weapons and an unshakeable belief in their 'civilising mission', the French proclaimed Tonkin a colony too, and Vietnam had become a French protectorate. In 1887 this was formalised and extended with the proclamation of an Indochinese Union of Vietnam, Laos and Cambodia: French Indochina had become a reality.

Predictably, the Vietnamese rejected French imperialism. A proud people who had resisted Chinese domination for two millennia were hardly likely to submit quietly to French rule. Meanwhile, in 1890 at a small hamlet in rural Vinh, Ho Chi Minh, the future leader of Vietnam's struggle for independence, was born.

In 1918 Ho travelled to Paris, and three years later joined the French Communist Party. By 1930 he had visited Moscow, become an agent of the Comintern, and formed the Indochinese Communist Party in Hong Kong. The French didn't know it yet, but the writing was already on the wall.

Ho Chi Minh in the field

Ho continued to organise his compatriots for independence throughout the war years and the Japanese occupation, which ended in 1945. Of course the communists weren't the only force opposed to French colonialism – Vietnamese of all political colours wanted their freedom – but there can be no doubt the communists were the best organised.

A French tank, abandoned in 1954 after the First Indochina War

Three Indochina Wars

Following the Japanese capitulation on 15 August 1945, events moved rapidly towards a series of three Indochina Wars. On 23 August Bao Dai, the last Nguyen Emperor, abdicated. Just 10 days later, on 2 September 1945, Ho Chi Minh declared Vietnamese independence in Hanoi.

This was unacceptable to the French, and in 1946 the First Indochina War began as France sought to reimpose colonial rule. The French fared badly, and in 1954 suffered a crushing defeat at the hands of Ho Chi Minh's greatest general, Vo Nguyen Giap, at Dien Bien Phu. Vietnam was subsequently divided at the 17th parallel, theoretically pending elections. North Vietnam, with its capital at Hanoi, was ruled by a communist regime under Ho Chi Minh. South Vietnam, with its capital at Saigon, was ruled by a pro-Western, Catholic strongman, Ngo Dinh Diem. In 1955 Diem refused to hold elections and, backed by Hanoi, Viet

Minh forces began armed attacks in the south. This event led to the start of the Second Indochina War – known to the Vietnamese as the 'American War', which would ravage the country for almost 20 years. In a misconceived attempt to contain communism, the United States first sent advisers to assist the southern regime in 1960. By 1965 the USAF had started regular bombing of the north, and US combat troops had landed at Danang in the south. By 1968 US troop strength had risen to more than half a million men, but that year's Tet Offensive by the Viet Cong sapped Washington's will to fight, and in 1973 the last US combat troops were withdrawn. Within two years, in April 1975, the North Vietnamese Army (NVA) had captured Saigon and Vietnam was once again unified by force.

Hanoi's victory led to the proclamation of the Socialist Republic of Vietnam. There was no bloodbath, but a sterile command economy was implemented and for more than a decade most Vietnamese suffered dire poverty and political oppression. This was compounded by the Third Indochina War (1978–79), when Vietnam invaded Cambodia to oust the murderous Khmer Rouge regime and was in turn invaded as a 'lesson' by Communist China.

Economic Growth

At the Sixth Congress of the Vietnamese Communist Party in 1986, the party leadership fretfully decided to launch the country on an ambitious programme of social and economic reform called *doi moi*. Collectivisation of land was rolled back, and a new emphasis was placed on the productivity and personal rights of the people. As a consequence, agricultural production increased and Vietnam became a major rice exporter. Political controls remain strict, however, and individual rights of expression remain limited. The economy still has its ups and downs, but tourism is becoming significant.

Historical Landmarks

258BC Vietnamese state called Au Lac established near present Hanoi.
207BC Chinese conquer Au Lac
AD40 Rebellion of the Trung Sisters
938 Battle at Bach Dang ends 1,000 years of Chinese domination.
1005 Buddhism established as major religion of Vietnam.
1471 Champa suffers crushing military defeat by Vietnam.
1516 Portuguese seafarers are first Westerners to arrive in Vietnam.
1539–1778 Trinh Lords dominate the north; Nguyen Lords rule the south.
1802–19 Emperor Gia Long establishes Nguyen dynasty at Hue.
1861 French forces capture Saigon.
1883 France establishes protectorate over Vietnam.
1890 Birth of Ho Chi Minh.
1930 Ho Chi Minh forms Indochina Communist Party.
1940 Japan occupies Vietnam, leaving French administration intact.
1945 Japan defeated; Ho Chi Minh declares independence.
1946 First Indochina War begins.
1954 French defeated, Vietnam divided at 17th parallel.
1955 Second Indochina War begins; first US aid to South Vietnam.
1968 US troop strength rises to 540,000.
1969 Ho Chi Minh dies aged 79.
1973 Washington and Hanoi sign cease-fire.
1975 NVA captures Saigon. Communist victory in the south.
1976 The Socialist Republic of Vietnam is declared.
1978 Vietnam invades Cambodia in Third Indochina War.
1979 China retaliates by short invasion of northern Vietnam.
1986 Sixth Party Congress embraces *doi moi* economic reforms.
1989 Vietnamese troops leave Cambodia.
1990 Peace talks with China; Vietnam establishes relations with the EU.
1994 US trade embargo lifted.
1995 Vietnam joins Association of Southeast Asian Nations (ASEAN).
1997–2000 Economic reforms stall; foreign investors pull out.
2003 Economy improves, tourism expands.

WHERE TO GO

Travel in Vietnam is anything but easy. After decades of war and with an economy that was subsequently throttled, the country's infrastructure – or lack of it – can test the most hardened traveller's patience. But Vietnam is truly one of those destinations where the inconveniences pale beside the remarkable, and where the beauty of its culture seduces all. The residue of warfare is now part of the country's tourism attractions, whether for the Cu Chi tunnels outside of the former Saigon or the rusting heaps at a Hanoi war museum. However, beyond the memories of war the bright tropical sun illuminates a coastline of serene, white-sand beaches and clear, blue waters, and mists veil forested mountains that are alive with exotic animals.

Northern Vietnam is anchored by Hanoi, an ancient city established nearly 1,000 years ago. The old villas and façades of the French colonial era give the city an ambience not found anywhere else in Asia. Beyond Hanoi, the provinces of the vast Red River Delta reflect the traditional agricultural culture on which the economy is based. And beyond the delta's plains, the cooler mountain regions, populated by hill tribes, ascend towards the west and Laos and north towards China.

Southwards, following the historical movement of the Viet people, the traveller finds a chain of coastal provinces washed by the South China Sea. In the old imperial city of Hue, an overwhelming sense of the past pervades the streets. The antiquities don't end here. In the lands of the ancient kingdom of Champa further south are decaying sanctuaries, temples and towers that testify to its conquest by the Viet

Cyclo drivers wait for passengers in the old city of Hoi An

people from the north. Then there is the city of Ho Chi Minh. Often still called Saigon, it is reviving its long-time image as the clichéd hustling-and-bustling city of people on the make and on the go. Where Hanoi is quiet, Ho Chi Minh is frenetic. If Hanoi is a city of earth tones, Ho Chi Minh is neon, all lit up in gaudy lights. The country has moved far beyond a century of foreign domination and war, and the traveller will find that Vietnam is a land of the ascending dragon and a place finally at peace.

HANOI

Hanoi is quite simply the most charming and traditional capital city in Southeast Asia. Although it was surprisingly little damaged by bombing during the Second Indochina War, when the country first began to open up after the communist seizure of power, years of political isolation and

The elegant, red-lacquered arch of Sunrise Bridge, on Ho Hoan Kiem

failed socialist economics had reduced the city to shabby penury. Today all that is changing, and things continue to improve. Hanoi has an entrancing mix of indigenous Sino-Vietnamese and French colonial architecture. Thankfully, the Vietnamese authorities have discovered the economic potential of Hanoi as a tourist magnet just in time to save the older parts of the city from the wrecking ball and the construction of soulless, high-rise buildings that disfigure so many other Southeast Asian cities. The people here are friendly, the food is excellent and varied, and the entertainment scene – while still not as active as in the former southern capital, Ho Chi Minh City – is livening up. Hanoi is also a city of culture *par excellence*, with many museums and art galleries, and a thriving artistic scene.

Hanoi, the Northern Capital

The area around Hanoi – the name means 'within the waters' after the city's close relationship with the Red River and numerous surrounding lakes – has been the site of Vietnam's capital for most of the last 2,000 years. In the 3rd century BC King Thuc Pan established the earliest Vietnamese capital at the citadel of Co Loa just north of the present-day city. Over 1,000 years later, when the Chinese were driven out and independence restored, General Ngo Quyen symbolically chose Hanoi as the site of the new Viet nation.

Subsequently in 1802 the first Nguyen Emperor, Gia Long, transferred the capital to Hue, but this was just a short-lived move. In 1902 France established Hanoi as the capital not just of Vietnam, but of all French Indochina. In 1954 the city became the capital of the communist north, and in 1976, following the defeat of the non-communist south, it was proclaimed capital of the reunited Socialist Republic of Vietnam. In many ways, and despite the independently-minded Saigonese, Hanoi remains the very heart of the Vietnamese nation.

Hanoi may be broadly divided into three districts – the **Old Quarter**, between the Song Hong (Red River) and the northern rim of Hoan Kiem Lake, **Central Hanoi** around the former French Quarter to the south of Hoan Kiem, and **Western Hanoi**, home to the Presidential Palace and Ho Chi Minh's Mausoleum. Beyond lie the city's sprawling suburbs.

The Old Quarter

Hanoi's historic **Old Quarter** is also known as **Ba Muoi Sau Pho Puong**, 'The 36 Streets'. This area, which is almost entirely devoted to commerce, dates back seven centuries to the time when a group of 36 guilds established themselves in the area, each centred on a particular street. Today many of the original street names survive, though few are still identified with a particular trade. Examples include **Hang Ma** or Paper Street, **Hang Bac** or Silver Street, **Hang Thiec** or Tin Street and **Hang Chieu** or Mat Street – of these only Hang Bac still continues in its original craft, specialising in the sale of jewellery.

The best way to see the Old Quarter is by walking, seeking out the most lively or fascinating sights, one of which is the lively **Dong Xuan Market**. Long the largest market in Hanoi, Dong Xuan was built in 1889. Sadly the old market burned down in 1994, but it has since been rebuilt and retains its original façade. Of particular note are the traditional **tube houses**, long, narrow commercial buildings designed to combine shop front, storage space and living quar-

A food seller in the Old Quarter

ters, which are extremely narrow and deep. Designed in this fashion six centuries ago to minimise a swingeing government tax on shop frontage, today they survive only in Hanoi and in the central port of Hoi An.

An ornate shutter in Den Bach Ma

While chiefly important as an area of commerce, the Old Quarter also has several important historic monuments. These include, on the eastern side of the quarter, **Cua O Quan Chuong** or the Gate of the Commander of the Garrison. This was built in 1749 and is now the sole surviving fortified gateway in Old Hanoi. Close by is **Den Bach Ma** or White Horse Temple. Established 1,100 years ago to commemorate the spirit of a white horse that is believed to protect the Old City, the present structure dates largely from the 18th century.

Central Hanoi

Ho Hoan Kiem, which means 'the lake of the restored sword' in Vietnamese, represents the historic heart of Old Hanoi. It was here that the revered national hero Le Loi was given a magic sword by a divine turtle that rose from the depth of the lake. After 10 years of warfare Le Loi, armed with this magic sword, led an uprising that succeeded in driving out the hated Chinese. Legend has it that a grateful Le Loi, by now enthroned as the Emperor Le Thai Tho, returned the sword to the divine turtle, which is still believed to guard the sacred weapon beneath the waters of the lake. In the middle of the

Every morning at 6am Radio Hanoi begins its programmes with a lyrical song:
Wherever we are at the four points of the compass,
Our hearts turn to Hanoi:
The Lake of the Restored Sword with its blue waters,
Which mirror the slanted shadow of Tortoise Tower.

lake a small pagoda, **Thap Rua** or Tortoise Tower, standing on a small islet, commemorates these events.

Today Ho Hoan Kiem remains a tranquil retreat from the hustle and bustle of the Old City to the north and the more upmarket boulevards of Downtown Hanoi to the south. At the northeastern corner of the lake stands the elegant Writing Brush Pillar, a tall stone column in the shape of a traditional brush pen engraved with Chinese characters which proclaim 'writing on a blue sky'. It was erected by the 19th-century scholar Nguyen Van Sieu. Close by, the graceful, red-lacquered arch of **The Huc**, or Sunrise Bridge, built in 1885, leads to a small island and to **Den Ngoc Son**, the Temple of the Jade Mound. Founded in the 14th century this splendid building was originally a Confucian temple. Between the 16th and 18th centuries it served as a pavilion for the Trinh Lords of Hanoi, while in the 19th century it was re-established as a Buddhist temple.

Nearby, on the eastern side of Pho Dinh Tien Hoang, is a fine old temple that has been converted to serve as an art gallery. Elsewhere the shop fronts along the northern and western sides of Hoa Koan Kiem house many galleries selling some really fine paintings – as well as, inevitably, some kitsch. No city in Southeast Asia has a better or more eclectic collection of galleries, with everything from traditional Vietnamese art to European-style paintings: the influence, in particular, of French Impressionism and even Russian

Socialist Realism is clearly discernible. This is a good area to stroll and shop, especially as there are plenty of small restaurants and cafés where iced beer and excellent Vietnamese coffee are available.

A real must for visitors to Hanoi is the **Water Puppet Theatre** at 57 Pho Dinh Tien Hoang – not far from the eastern end of The Huc Bridge. The art of water-puppetry or *roi nuoc* is unique to Vietnam and is believed to have originated in the Red River Delta more than 1,000 years ago. The puppets are carved from a hard, water-resistant wood to represent both traditional rural lifestyles, such as farmers and bullocks, and mythical creatures like dragons and phoenixes. The puppeteers stand concealed, waist-deep in water, and use a complex system of ropes and pulleys to manipulate their charges with quite remarkable skill, while a traditional orchestra plays accompanying music.

Hanoi's Water Puppet Theatre

To the east a path winds beneath shady trees, and to the west of the lake groups of old men play chess, and mixed groups of men and women practise *tai chi.* Not far along Hang Trong, a road leading west from the lake, stands **St Joseph's Cathedral**, built by the French and consecrated in 1886.

South of the lake lies the commercial heart of Hanoi, an area originally built by

The Parisian-style Opera House is now a municipal theatre

the French, which is now rapidly being modernised. Although it is dominated by broad, east–west boulevards and shopfronts, a small temple is tucked away on a small side street at 73 Quan Su. This is **Chuan Quan Su**, or the Ambassadors' Pagoda. Unfortunately little of the original 17th-century structure survives, and what we see today dates mainly from the 1930s. Once a lodging for ambassadors from neighbouring Buddhist countries, it remains an active Buddhist centre.

Dominating the central Hanoi skyline on Pho Hoa Lo a high-rise tower marks the former site of **Hoa Lo**, a prison built by the French in 1896, in which thousands of Vietnamese political prisoners were incarcerated during the colonial period. Today it is better known to most Western visitors as the '**Hanoi Hilton**', the nickname it was given by US prisoners of war held here during the Second Indochina War. In the mid-1990s the prison was demolished to make way for a shopping mall and hotel complex, but a small part of the prison was preserved as a museum exhibiting a few cells, stocks and a guillotine.

Further east on busy Ngo Quyen the former **Residence of the Governor of Tonkin** is an elegant colonial building dating from 1918. Nearby, at the eastern end of Pho Trang Thi, the restored **Opera House** now functions as a municipal theatre. This magnificent building, styled after the neo-baroque Paris Opera, was regarded as the most sophisticated expression of French culture in all Indochina.

East of the Opera House, by the Red River embankment, a number of museums include the **Revolution Museum** (open daily 8–11.30am, 1.30–4.30pm; admission fee), the **Geology Museum** (open Mon–Sat 8am–noon, 1.30–4.30pm; admission fee) and the **History Museum** (open Fri–Wed 8.15–11.45am, 1.30–5pm; admission fee). This last, founded in the 1930s by the Ecole Française d'Extrême Orient, houses an impressive collection of artefacts.

Western Hanoi

The delightful **Tran Quoc Pagoda** is picturesquely situated on an island west of the causeway separating Truc Bach Lake from the much larger Ho Tay, or West Lake. It's one of Vietnam's oldest temples, dating back to the 6th-century Early Ly Dynasty. A stone stele from 1639, standing in the temple grounds, records that it was relocated in the 15th

Tran Quoc Pagoda, one of the oldest temples in Vietnam

century to protect it from the encroaching Red River. In its current form it dates from 1842.

To the east lie the still waters of **Truc Bach** or White Silk Lake. During the 18th century the Trinh Lords built a summer palace here, which later became a place of detention for disobedient royal concubines; they would be set to weaving fine white silk. Southeast of the causeway another lovely temple, **Quan Thanh**, stands in shady grounds. Endowed in the early 11th century by the founder of the Early Ly Dynasty, Ly Thai To, this temple is dedicated to Tran Vo, guardian spirit of the city of Hanoi. An image of this Taoist divinity, accompanied by his symbols of power – the turtle

Vietnamese Temple Architecture

A Vietnamese pagoda consists of several rooms. At the front are doors that are opened only for major religious festivals. Behind these doors lie a front hall, a central hall and the main altar room, usually arranged in ascending levels. Behind the temple, or to the side, are living quarters for monks or nuns. There will also usually be one or more subsidiary altar rooms specifically dedicated to the rites of ancestor worship, where funerary tablets and pictures of deceased monks and relatives are displayed.

Vietnamese temples are generally distinguished by their lavish use of dragon motifs. These are not the dangerous creatures of Western mythology, but the noble and beneficial dragons of imperial Chinese tradition. Look for them outside, on the eaves and the apex of main roofs; inside they may be twined around supporting pillars, holding up altars, and guarding doorways. Other decorative images to look for include Buddhist swastika motifs and the yin-yang symbol of Taoism symbolising the duality, or male and female elements of existence. Chinese characters, too, although long abandoned by modern written Vietnamese, remain an essential part of the Viet spirit world.

and the snake – cast in 1677, dominates the main altar.

Keeping guard outside the Ho Chi Minh Mausoleum

Further south along Duong Hung Vuong, by the **Hanoi Botanical Gardens**, stands the **Presidential Palace**. This particularly fine example of French colonial architecture was built in 1906 as the Palace of the Governor General of Indo-china. Although it is closed to the public, it's possible to walk through the palace grounds along a clearly indicated route to visit **Ho Chi Minh's House**, an unassuming residence on stilts where Ho spent the last decade of his life. The atmosphere is distinctly ascetic, with a small garden and pond. On the first floor the bedroom and study are preserved as Ho left them, with a few simple possessions.

Immediately to the south the austere **Ho Chi Minh Mausoleum** faces the **National Assembly** across Ba Dinh Square. It was here that Ho read the Vietnamese Declaration of Independence on 2 September 1945, and it was here that he was entombed after his death on 2 September 1969, despite his wish to be cremated and scattered across the country. The mausoleum, built in Stalinist style and modelled on the Mausoleum of Lenin in Red Square, was completed in 1975 using marble, granite and rare woods brought from all over Vietnam. Visitors may enter and briefly view

Ho's embalmed body. Respectful dress is a requirement, and photography is strictly prohibited.

A short distance to the south is the celebrated **Chua Mot Cot** (One Pillar Pagoda), a small but elegant structure erected by King Ly Thai Tong in the 11th century. The single column on which the pagoda rests rises from a tranquil lotus-filled pond. The pipal (bo tree) growing by the temple was planted by President Nehru of India during a state visit in 1958 and is said to be an offshoot of the tree under which the Buddha attained enlightenment. The attractive facade of the nearby **Dien Huu Pagoda** opens on to a quiet garden courtyard. Many Vietnamese visitors come for the acupuncture treatment with which the temple is associated.

Dominating both pagodas is the **Ho Chi Minh Museum** (open daily, except Mon and Fri, 8–11.30am, 1.30–4pm; admission fee) which opened on 19 May 1990, the 100th

Chua Mot Cot, perched on a single pillar, is an 11th-century pagoda

anniversary of Ho's birth. Exhibits portray aspects of Ho's life and the course of the Vietnamese Revolution, and include the personal effects of 'Uncle Ho'.

East of Chua Mot Cot lies Dien Bien Phu, a boulevard of shady trees and elegant colonial buildings. Here you will find the **Army Museum** (open daily 8–11.30am, 1.30–4.30pm; admission fee). Well-documented displays of Vietnamese military history feature wars against the Chinese, French and Americans. The museum courtyard delimits the southwest corner of the **Citadel**, formerly the centre of administration in pre-colonial times and today a restricted military area. **Cot Co**, or the Flag Tower, which is the most interesting surviving feature of the Citadel, is open to the public and well worth the climb for the magnificent views over the city to the Song Hong and the historic **Long Bien Bridge**.

The Socialist Republic of Vietnam flag flies over Cot Co

Nearby Nguyen Thai Hoc is home to the **National Fine Arts Museum** (open Tues–Sun 8–11am, 1.30–4pm; admission fee) providing exhibitions of art history from the Dong Son period, through the Kingdom of Champa and the pre-colonial Vietnamese dynasties, to contemporary times.

Van Mieu

South of Nguyen Thai Hoc is the much smaller Van Mieu Road that leads to **Van Mieu**, or the Temple of Literature. Founded in 1070 by King Ly Thanh Tong, the temple was

Confucius presides over the Sanctuary in Van Mieu

originally dedicated both to Confucius and to Chu Cong, a Chinese sage who conceived some of the teachings that Confucius developed five centuries later. The tradition of Confucian education flourished at the Temple of Literature, and in 1484 the first stele bearing the names of doctoral graduates was erected. The last examinations to be held at Van Mieu were conducted in 1915.

Entry to the temple complex is through **Van Mieu Gate**. The layout, based on that of the temple at Qufu in China where Confucius was born, consists of a succession of five walled courtyards. The first two, joined by **Dai Trung Mon** or Great Middle Gate, are carefully maintained gardens where locals come to paint, read or just talk. The third courtyard is reached via **Khue Van Cac**, or the Pavilion of the Constellation of Literature, a fine double-roofed gateway built in 1805. Here the visitor will find the **Garden of Stelae**, containing 82 stone memorials mounted on the backs of tortoises, each listing the names and brief biographical details of graduates of Van Mieu dating back to the 15th century.

Entry to the fourth courtyard, or Courtyard of the Sages, is via **Dai Thanh Mon**, or the Gate of the Great Synthesis. It was here, in the **Great House of Ceremonies**, that in times past the king would make offerings at the **Altar to Confucius** while new university graduates would kneel and prostrate themselves to pay respect. Behind the Great House of the Ceremonies is the **Sanctuary**, with statues of Confucius and his leading disciples including Manh Tu, better known as Mencius. The fifth and final courtyard contains the **Lieu Hanh Shrine**, dedicated to the goddess who is one of the Four Immortals honoured in Vietnamese tradition. A short distance to the southwest of Van Mieu is **Dao Quan Bich Cau**, or the Bich Cau Taoist temple. One of the most attractive structures in Hanoi, Bich Cau was last restored in 1896.

DAY TRIPS FROM HANOI

There are a number of worthwhile attractions in the vicinity of Hanoi, but they are scattered at all points of the compass at varying distances from the city. The best solution if you wish to explore the area is to stay in the capital and travel by taxi or bus to these destinations, perhaps combining two or three in a day if they are in the same general direction.

North of Hanoi

The first known independent Viet kingdom was created in 258BC when King An Duong established his capital at **Co Loa** 16km (26 miles) north of present-day Hanoi. There is little left of the original city, but a half-day trip to Co Loa Citadel is well worth the effort. An Duong built his capital within three concentric ramparts, which spiralled like the shell of a

Incense sticks drying on temple steps in Co Loa

A fisherman near Thai Nguyen

snail, and these are still just visible today. Close to the Citadel's former south gateway, a large pipal tree shades **Den My Chau**, a temple dedicated to An Duong's daughter, princess My Chau. Nearby **Den An Duong Vuong** is dedicated primarily to King An Duong, but also to the magical Golden Turtle Kim Quy. The terrace of this temple rests on six turned and lacquered pillars that support a long roof with curving eaves.

The town of **Thai Nguyen**, 76km (48 miles) north of Hanoi, is notable for its excellent **Museum of the Nationalities of Vietnam** (open Tues–Sun 7–11am, 2–5.30pm; admission fee). If you are interested in Vietnam's many colourful minorities, a visit is well worth the journey. The exhibits include everyday artefacts, costumes, photographs and video presentations, displayed in five large rooms divided by linguistic groups. The Mon-Khmer Room, recently redesigned, is particularly fascinating. The museum is in the centre of town.

East of Hanoi

The Song Hong Delta is well known for handicraft production, and several small villages within easy reach of Hanoi are traditionally associated with particular crafts. About

13km (8 miles) southeast of the capital on the left bank of the Song Hong the settlement of **Bat Trang** is renowned for its blue and white ceramics. There are around 2,000 families in Bat Trang, managing no fewer than 800 kilns. The village of **Van Phuc**, about 8km (5 miles) southwest of the capital on Route 6 to Hoa Binh, is famous for its silk production. **So**, a small village about 12km (7½ miles) further out on the same road, is known for producing hand-made noodles. **Dong Ky** village, about 15km (9 miles) northeast of the capital on Route 1 to Bac Ninh, is celebrated for its woodcarving. Visitors are always welcome at all these craft villages, and most tour companies in Hanoi are able to arrange short tours.

South and West of Hanoi

Chua Huong, or the Perfume Pagoda, established by the Trinh Lords in the 17th and 18th centuries, is set in the mountains some 60km (38 miles) southwest of Hanoi. It's possible to drive directly to Chua Huong, but the most popular way to go is by boat from Duc Khe on the Yen River. The river trip, winding through outstandingly beautiful countryside, takes around 2 hours, after which you have to walk about 4km (2½ miles) to the temple complex.

Chua Thay (Pagoda of the Teacher) is situated about 40km (25 miles) southwest of Hanoi on the shores of Long Tri Lake in Ha Tay Province. It's also known as **Thien Phuc Tu**, or the Heavenly Blessing Pagoda, and is dedicated to Thich Ca or Sakyamuni Buddha. To the right of the main altar stands a statue of King Ly Nhan Tong (1072–1127), during whose reign the pagoda was constructed, and to the left a statue of Tu Dao Hanh, the monk who first managed the establishment

Chua Thay contains more than 100 religious statues, including the two largest in Vietnam, each weighing more than 1,000kg (1 ton).

and was also a teacher and doctor to the local residents – hence the name of the pagoda. Tu Dao Hanh is said to have been a master water-puppeteer, and demonstrations of this ancient skill are given at the temple during the annual festival that takes place on the 5th to 7th days of the third lunar month.

Nearby **Tay Phuong**, or the Western Pagoda, lies some 6km (4 miles) to the west. Perched on top of a hill said to resemble a buffalo, Tay Phuong dates from the 8th century and is celebrated for its collection of more than 70 wooden statues representing both Buddhist and Confucian deities.

FURTHER AFIELD IN THE NORTH

Just over 100km (63 miles) east of Hanoi is **Haiphong**, Vietnam's main port and fourth largest city. An important industrial centre, Haiphong suffered badly from USAF bombing during the Vietnam War, and the poorly rebuilt suburbs remain unattractive and depressing. The town centre is much more appealing, however, and retains a distinct French colonial flavour in its buildings, notably the rose-coloured **Haiphong Museum** (open Tues, Wed and Sun 8–10am, 2–4pm) on Dien Bien Phuc Street, the pink **Haiphong Theatre** on Hoang Van Thu, and the 19th-century **Cathedral** by the Tam Bac River. The 17th-century **Du Hang Pagoda**, located on Pho Chua Hang to the south of the railway tracks, is worth a visit for its elaborate Buddhist architecture. Close by, on Nguyen Cong Tru Street, stands **Dinh Hang Kenh**, a traditional communal house raised on ironwood columns facing an ornamental lake.

A 3-hour ferry ride to the northeast leads to **Halong City**. Not everyone's idea of an ideal holiday destination, this resort is designed to appeal to locals and to visitors from nearby China. Karaoke bars and sleazy nightlife flourish, but these rather dubious attractions in no way detract from the unexpected beauty of the hundreds of islands dotting the nearby waters of the Gulf of Tonkin.

Halong Bay

In Vietnamese *ha long* means 'descending dragon', and legend has it that **Halong Bay** was formed by a celestial dragon which plunged into the Gulf of Tonkin, creating thousands of limestone outcrops by lashing its tail. More than 2,000 craggy, rugged islets lie scattered across the huge bay, making an excursion by boat a truly memorable experience. Boats can be chartered locally at the harbour in Hong Gai; alternatively almost any travel agent in Halong City or even in Hanoi will make arrangements for a tour. The most spectacular islands and dramatic caves lie in the western part of the bay. A full day tour of the islands is the best option, though shorter trips are possible – lunch or dinner on board, generally consisting of fresh seafood, is highly recommended, but catering arrangements should be made beforehand.

Memorable excursion: a tourist cruise round dramatic Halong Bay

One way to see Halong Bay while avoiding Halong City is via the island of **Cat Ba**. The easiest way to get there is by air-conditioned express boat from Haiphong. There are also two slow ferries each day. The route to Cat Ba cuts across the **Bach Dang River** estuary where the Vietnamese routed invading Chinese forces in AD938 and destroyed an attacking Mongol fleet in 1288. Boats dock at Cat Ba Town, the only settlement of any size, where it is possible to stay overnight. Boats may be chartered to explore Halong Bay to the north, or the smaller but picturesque **Lan Ha Bay** to the northeast.

About half of Cat Ba Island is taken up by Cat Ba National Park, home to many species of birds, such as hawks, hornbills and cuckoos, and more than 20 mammals, including the only known population of Golden-headed Leaf Monkey.

Beyond Halong Bay unlikely limestone outcrops stud the sea northwards all the way to the Chinese frontier by way of **Ba Tu Long Bay**. A charter to this very scenic and unspoiled area can be arranged from Halong City and takes about 5 hours each way.

The Northwest

Rugged northwestern Vietnam offers some of the most beautiful scenery in the whole country, as well as a chance to meet minority hill peoples with cultural identities and languages quite different from the dominant Vietnamese. The most interesting way to reach this area is via the single-line narrow-gauge track leading to Kunming, the capital of China's Yunnan Province. It's also possible to travel by bus or taxi. There's little of interest in the border town of **Lao Cai**, not least because the People's Liberation Army dynamited the whole city in 1979 as part of China's 'lesson' to Vietnam for invading Cambodia and overthrowing the mur-

Sa Pa: built by the French as a hill station, now a popular tourist centre

derous Khmer Rouge regime. Today it's just a place to have a meal and spend the night before heading on into the hills. About the only local diversion is to visit the international frontier and watch people crossing in and out of China via the busy **Coc Leu Bridge**.

The hill town of **Sa Pa** is 38km (24 miles) from Lao Cai by way of a narrow road that climbs slowly into the hills. Developed in 1922 as a hill station, Sa Pa lies at an elevation of 1,600m (5,200ft) and is pleasantly cool during the hot season and decidedly cold during the winter months. Besides the beautiful scenery and cool climate, this small market town affords the visitor an opportunity to sample the temperate fruits and vegetables grown here, and to interact with the local hill peoples.

Most people living in Sa Pa town are ethnic Vietnamese, while the minorities live in small villages on the outskirts. It's possible to walk to some of these settlements, one of the most

Hmong women in Sa Pa market

popular being the Hmong village of **Cat Cat**, just 3km (2 miles) distant. There are also Dao, Red Dao and Tay villages within about 12km (7 miles), but most visitors make do with Sa Pa's colourful **weekend market**. This event, which is of social as well as commercial importance to the locals, runs between noon on Saturday and noon on Sunday, with hill peoples flocking in from the surrounding villages to trade and exchange gossip. Many women dress in their finest clothing, sporting leggings, embroidered skirts and jackets, heavy silver jewellery and elaborate headdresses.

If you are interested in the natural wilderness and military history, then a visit to the former battlefield of **Dien Bien Phu** is certainly worthwhile. It's an 18-hour journey by road from Hanoi, but there are also three flights a week. In 1954 Vietnam's celebrated military commander General Vo Nguyen Giap successfully besieged and then reduced the French garrison occupying the valley. More than 2,000 soldiers were killed and another 11,000 taken prisoner. This decisive Vietnamese victory effectively brought the First Indochina War to an end. Today the old battlefield has become a tourist attraction. The former HQ of the French commander, Colonel de Castries, has been rebuilt and some rusting French tanks and heavy artillery pieces are collected nearby.

THE CENTRE

The Vietnamese sometimes liken their country to a shoulder-pole with a pannier at either end. The panniers – that is, the Red River Delta around Hanoi and the Mekong Delta south of Ho Chi Minh City – are the most densely populated regions of the country and tend to overshadow the 'pole'. Yet the centre has a flavour quite distinct from that of either the north or the south.

The city of Hue was once the imperial capital and remains the most staunchly Buddhist region in the entire country. Just south of Danang, Vietnam's fourth largest city, the ancient and picturesque riverine port of Hoi An has been lovingly restored. South of Danang all the way down the central coast to Phan Tiet stand complexes of brick towers, silent reminders of the ancient Cham civilisation which once flourished in this area. The best beaches in Vietnam are to be found in this central area, notably at Nha Trang and Mui Ne. Finally, a short distance inland in the cool Central Highlands, the old French hill station of Dalat has become a major tourist destination.

Hue

The former imperial city of **Hue** is the most significant cultural monument in Vietnam. It is also a place of sublime beauty and, despite having been badly damaged during the 1968 Tet Offensive, it remains a magical place. Renowned throughout the country for the elegance of its women and its sophisticated royal cuisine,

A ceremonial urn in the Forbidden Purple City, Hue

Hue lies at the very heart of Vietnamese cultural tradition. The **Song Huong** (Perfume River) flows through the city, while the surrounding countryside is studded with royal tombs built during the time of the Nguyen Kings.

Dominating the Hue skyline is the 37-m (120-ft) **Cot Co** or Flag Tower, first erected in 1809. Cot Co became internationally famous on 31 January 1968, when communist forces seized Hue Citadel and ran their yellow-starred banner up its tall mast. For the next 25 days Hue suffered badly as the Americans and their South Vietnamese allies struggled to recapture the city. The damage was immense, but in 1993 UNESCO declared Hue a World Heritage Site, and restoration and conservation work has since continued with considerable success.

Originally part of the Kingdom of Champa, Hue first became part of Vietnam in 1306 when King Jaya Sinhavarman III ceded it to Hanoi as dowry in a royal marriage. In 1558 the city became capital of the Nguyen rulers of south-central Vietnam. In 1802 Nguyen Anh, the last of the

Music Ancient and Modern

Traditional Vietnamese music combines indigenous techniques thought to date back to the Dong Son period, with Chinese influences and, through the Hindu Kingdom of Champa, Indian musical forms. The resultant mix, which is technically very complex, is based on a five-note scale. Traditional Vietnamese musical groups include wind instruments, string instruments, zithers and drums; they are often accompanied by song. An excellent place to see and hear traditional Vietnamese music is at the Van Mieu Temple of Literature in Hanoi. Contemporary music in Vietnam has inevitably been influenced by Chinese, Thai and Western pop music. The resultant Viet Pop is known as 'Yellow Music'.

The Ngan Gate: one of the 10 entrances to Hue's moated Citadel

Nguyen Lords, defeated his rivals in Hanoi and proclaimed Hue the imperial capital of a united Vietnam – at the same time proclaiming himself Emperor Gia Long. In 1805 he strengthened his position further by ordering the building of **Kinh Thanh**, Hue's massive moated Citadel.

Entry to the Citadel is by way of 10 fortified gates, each of which is reached by a low, arched stone bridge across the moat. In imperial times a cannon would sound at 5am and 9pm to mark the opening and closing of the gates. The area within the Citadel comprises three enclosures, the first of which was formerly used to accommodate various royal ministries and which today constitutes a pleasant area of parks, gardens and quiet residential districts. Here may be found the **Nine Holy Cannons**, kept in buildings flanking the gates on either side of the Flag Tower.

A second moat and defensive wall within the Citadel guard the **Hoang Thanh**, or Yellow City, deliberately modelled on the Forbidden City in Beijing. This inner city has four gates, the chief of which is called **Cua Ngo Mon** or Meridian Gate. This majestic structure, built during the reign of Emperor Minh Mang in 1833, is among the finest surviving examples of Nguyen architecture. The central entrance, reserved exclusively for the emperor, is flanked by smaller passages for the use of mandarins and court officials; these in turn are flanked by two much wider passages intended for the royal elephants. Above the Cua Ngo Mon rises **Five Phoenix Watchtower** where the emperor sat in state during important ceremonies.

Beyond the Ngo Mon Gate **Kim Thuy Kieu**, or the Bridge of Golden Waters, leads between lotus-filled ponds to **Thai Hoa Dien**, the Hall of Supreme Harmony. This was the throne room of the Nguyen Kings, and is the best preserved of Hue's surviving palaces. Built by Gia Long in 1805, its yellow-tiled roof is supported by 80 massive wooden columns, lacquered a deep red and decorated with imperial golden dragons.

Immediately behind the throne room **Dai Cung Mon**, the Great Golden Gate, leads through to **Tu Cam Thanh**, the Forbidden Purple City. This was once the sole preserve of the emperor, his queen, his many concubines and female palace servants. No man but the king could set foot here on pain of death – imperial sons were banished when they reached puberty, and the only non-females permitted within the inner sanctum were palace eunuchs. In imperial times the Purple City consisted of more than

Young women in traditional dress on the steps of Thien Mu Pagoda

60 buildings arranged around 20 courtyards, but it was seriously damaged by fire in 1947 and all but destroyed during the Tet Offensive of 1968. Restoration work based on surviving photographs and plans was begun in the mid-1990s and is now well under way.

The seven-storey Thap Phuoc Duyen at Thien Mu

Around Hue

On the north bank of the Perfume River, about 4km (2½ miles) southwest of the Citadel, stands the celebrated **Thien Mu Pagoda**, long considered a symbol for the City of Hue. Originally founded in 1601 by Lord Nguyen Hoang, the most striking feature of the temple is a 21-m (68-ft) high octagonal tower, the seven-storey **Thap Phuoc Duyen**, or the Tower of the Source of Happiness, which stands on a small hillock overlooking the Perfume River. Two pavilions close by house a stone stele erected in 1715 which records the history of Buddhism in Hue, and a large bronze bell, cast in 1710, which weighs over 2,000kg (2 tons). The sound of this bell is said to reach over 10km (6 miles), and in times past could clearly be heard in Hue city.

Just west of Thien Mieu, **Van Mieu**, the Confucian Temple of Literature, was founded by Gia Long in 1808 in clear imitation of the better-known Temple of Literature in Hanoi.

Song Huong, the Perfume River, rolls lazily below Van Mieu

It's an interesting side visit from Thien Mieu, offering fine views of the Perfume River, but it cannot compare to its northern rival.

On the south bank of the Perfume River, beyond the former French quarter now known as Khu Pho Moi (New City) is **Dan Nam Giao**, or the Altar of Heaven. During the years of Hue's primacy this was the most important religious centre in the country, though today there isn't a lot to see beyond a series of three raised terraces. The first, square terrace is said to represent humanity, the second, also square, to represent earth, while the third, round terrace represents heaven. Here, every three years between 1806 and 1945, the Nguyen Emperors reaffirmed the legitimacy of their rule through a series of elaborate sacrifices to the Emperor of Heaven – once again mirroring Chinese imperial practice.

Another imperial relic is **Ho Quyen**, the Royal Arena of the Nguyen Kings, 4km (2½ miles) southwest of Hue near the village of Phuong Duc. Tigers were forced to fight elephants in this amphitheatre, and the elephant, which was synonymous with imperial power, was invariably victorious. This result was achieved in a rather unsporting fashion, by de-clawing the tiger and sewing its mouth shut before battle began. The last fight was held in 1904.

Any visit to Hue should certainly include a boat trip on the beautiful **Perfume River**. Boats are readily available for hire, either for a relaxing trip in the vicinity of Hue, or for a longer journey upstream to the tombs of Minh Mang and Gia Long. The clarity of the water, together with the profusion of colourful craft and boat women sporting *non la* conical hats, all contribute to the magical effect.

The Imperial Tombs

Scattered across the countryside to the south and west of the city, the **Tombs of the Nguyen Emperors** are, together with the Citadel, Hue's greatest attraction. The Vietnamese word for tomb is *lang*, and this is used as a standard prefix for all the royal tombs. Although 13 rulers sat on the imperial throne between 1802 and 1945, only seven have their own royal mausoleum. These seven tombs, all of which have features of outstanding architectural merit, are often strikingly different and several, if not all, are worthy of a visit.

Lang Duc Duc is the tomb nearest to Hue, but also one of the hardest to find. Located just south of the railway line on Tan Lang Lane, it was erected in 1899 and has recently undergone restoration. Duc Duc, the nephew and adopted son of Tu Duc, reigned for a mere three days in 1883. Dethroned as a result of court intrigue, he later starved to death in prison. According to legend, he was being carried to a common burial when the mat in which he was being carried split open, so he was summarily buried at the location of the current tomb. Six years later his son, Thanh Thai

(1889–1907), became emperor and erected a mausoleum for Duc Duc over the spot where he had been buried.

Lang Tu Duc, built between 1864 and 1867, is perhaps the most exquisitely designed of the Nguyen tombs. About 6km (4 miles) southwest of Hue, set in the hills of Thuy Xuan district, this splendid mausoleum was built by Emperor Tu Duc (1848–83). It's built on a grand scale, but with great attention to detail. Designed by Tu Duc himself, the mausoleum is set amidst fragrant pines and frangipani trees, surrounded by tranquil ponds. It was Tu Duc's habit to recline here in the gorgeous **Xung Khiem Pavilion** composing poetry, reflecting on the nature of existence, or dallying with his wives and concubines.

Lang Dong Khanh, the mausoleum of Emperor Dong Khanh (1885–88), lies slightly southeast of Lang Tu Duc. Like Duc Duc, Dong Khanh was the nephew and adopted son

Lang Tu Duc, the most beautiful of the Nguyen mausoleums

of the childless Tu Duc. His mausoleum, the smallest of the Nguyen Tombs, is in exquisite taste and unusually well preserved. The exterior of the main temple is traditionally Vietnamese, but the interior shows signs of French cultural influence already influencing imperial tastes, notably in engravings of Napoleon and the Battle of Waterloo which hang from the red-lacquered ironwood pillars supporting the roof.

Nguyen Emperor Dong Khanh

Lang Thieu Tri, the mausoleum of Emperor Thieu Tri (1841–47), is one of the smaller tombs, lacking the usual walled gardens. To the west is the actual tomb, while to the east a finely executed temple stands almost entirely surrounded by small lakes. It's located about 1.5km (1 mile) from Lang Tu Duc, south of the Perfume River.

Lang Khai Dinh, the mausoleum of Emperor Khai Dinh (1916–25), is about 10km (6 miles) to the southwest of Hue. Built between 1920 and 1931, the tomb rises through a series of stairs and courtyards on the side of a low hill. The architect clearly sought to combine Vietnamese and French cultural traditions in this tomb, and the result – while verging on the kitsch – is both unique and unforgettable.

Lang Minh Mang, the mausoleum of Emperor Minh Mang (1820–41), lies on the left bank of the Perfume River about 12km (7 miles) from Hue. Planned in Minh Mang's lifetime but executed after his death, the complex – which includes elegant portals, bridges, lakes and pavilions, as

The impressive mausoleum of Emperor Minh Mang

well as the **Sung An Temple** dedicated to the Emperor and Empress – is perhaps the most impressive of all the Nguyen Tombs.

Lang Gia Long, the mausoleum of the first Nguyen Emperor Gia Long (1802–20), is also located on the left bank of the Perfume River, a 20-minute boat ride and short walk south of the Minh Mang ferry crossing. Remote from Hue and severely damaged during the Second Indochina War, this tomb is visited by relatively few people. It's worth the journey, though, and once restored will doubtless become a more familiar destination. For the present, take a local guide.

South of Hue

Unless you are a military buff or a veteran of the Second Indochina War, there's little to see to the immediate north of Hue. The provinces around the former Demilitarised Zone are among the poorest in Vietnam, with nothing in the way of cultural and historic sites, but a good deal to offer – at least off the beaten track – in terms of 'UXO', or unexploded ordinance. Unless entering or exiting the country by way of the Lao Bao crossing to neighbouring Laos, there is little to draw the visitor to these regions.

South of Hue is another matter. The road from Hue to Danang is among the most beautiful in the country, running past extensive lagoons with dense bird populations at **Thuy**

Tu and **Cau Hai** before meeting the sea at Lang Co and palm-fringed **Canh Duong Beach**. This is one of the prettiest and most relaxing strands in Vietnam, and as yet it has not been overdeveloped.

Beyond Lang Co the road climbs steeply to cross a spur of the Annamese Cordillera that juts into the South China Sea. This is the famous **Deo Hai Van**, or the Pass of the Clouds, so called because the 500-m (1,625-ft) high pass is often swathed in clouds and mist. When there is clear weather, the views are remarkable. Until 1306, Hai Van formed the frontier between Vietnam and the Kingdom of Champa, and the pass remains strategically important to the present day. It is also the geographic and climatic frontier between northern and southern Vietnam. To the north the winters are markedly colder and sometimes drier, while to the south winters tend to be warm and wet.

The road from Hue to Danang crosses the scenic Hai Van Pass

Danang

Vietnam's fourth largest city and site of the country's third international airport, **Danang** has adequate accommodation and a few good seafood restaurants, but – with the exception of its remarkable Cham Museum – lacks any intrinsic interest and is really just an industrial seaport. Fortunately there's no need to stay there, as just a short drive to the south lies the delightful old town of Hoi An, a riverine port bursting with history and noted both for its fine arts and equally distinguished cuisine.

➤ **Bao Tang Cham** (Cham Museum; open daily 7am–5pm; admission fee) is located on the northern bank of Danang's Han River. Founded in 1915 by the Ecole Française d'Extrême Orient, this unique cultural treasure trove is currently in need of restoration, but remains a must-see destination for its unique collection of Cham statuary and bas-reliefs. Figures from the pantheon of Hindu deities, including Vishnu, Shiva, Uma, Ganesh and Nandi are a recurrent theme, as is the female breast, an important icon in Cham religious art. Perhaps most famous of all the carvings on display is the exquisite dancing *apsara* from the Cham capital, Tra Kieu, in the northwest corner of Gallery Three.

Marble Mountain, about 7km (4 miles) south of Danang, contains a series of caverns that have long housed a series of shrines dedicated to Buddha or to Confucius. Today the area is swamped with stone-carving factories, and unless you wish to acquire a one-

Apsara dancer from Tra Kieu, in Danang's Cham Museum

tonne marble lion or Madonna it's probably best to avoid this heavily over-commercialised site.

China Beach stretching some 30km (18 miles) south of Danang was once a favourite Rest and Recreation area for US servicemen during the Second Indochina War. Today it's mainly a playground for local tourists, but has little to offer in terms of snorkelling or other watersports. Large stretches are all but deserted, and it's a good place to sunbathe and swim, though with relatively few facilities.

Boats on the Thu Bon River under Cam Nam Bridge in Hoi An

Hoi An

Located on the Thu Bon River 30km (18 miles) south of Danang, **Hoi An** has far more appeal than it's larger northern neighbour. During the time of the Nguyen Lords and even under the first Nguyen Emperors, Hoi An – then called Faifo – was an important port, visited regularly by shipping from Europe and all over the East. By the mid-19th century, however, the progressive silting up of the Thu Bon River and the development of nearby Danang combined to make Hoi An into a backwater. The result is a delightful old town with many of its historical monuments preserved, a place where the visitor may linger and explore for several days.

Hoi An is renowned for its **Traditional Houses**, most of which are found along Tran Phu, Nguyen Tai Hoc and Bach Dang Streets, next to the waterfront. Although generally still inhabited, these old mercantile homes are open to visitors on payment of a small fee. Best-known is **Tan Ky House**, a fine example of an 18th-century Sino-Viet shop-house built around a tiny central courtyard. It is distinguished by the elegant 'crab shell' ceiling and the exquisite mother-of-pearl inlay Chinese poetry hanging from the columns that support the roof. Nearby **Phung Hung House** has been home to the same family for eight generations, traditionally traders in perfumed woods and spices from Vietnam's Central Highlands. Supported by 80 hardwood columns, this building shows Chinese influence in the gallery and shuttered windows; the delicate glass skylights are Japanese in style.

The Hoa, or Overseas Chinese merchants, who dominated the commerce of Hoi An identified themselves with their native provinces, and built **Assembly Halls** to act as community centres and places of worship. Five distinct Overseas Chinese communities lived in Hoi An – Fujian, Guangdong, Hainan, Chaozhou and Hakka – and all except the latter had their own assembly hall (though the Hakka were able to participate in the **Chinese All Community Assembly**). All five

The Fujian Assembly Hall in Hoi An

halls survive today in Hoi An, and all are well worth visiting, though the **Fujian Assembly Hall**, founded in the late 17th century, is probably the most interesting. A large model of a wooden junk standing near the central altar serves to remind members of their cultural origins and how they came to Hoi An in the first place.

Hoi An also has a number of small but interesting temples. These include **Chua Ong**, also known as **Chua Quan Cong**, centrally located on Tran Phu Street, which was established in 1653 and is dedicated to Quan Cong, a member of the Taoist pantheon who brings good luck and protects travellers. **Chuc Thanh Pagoda**, about 1km (½ mile) north of the town

A driver wheels his cyclo past one of Hoi An's art galleries

centre, is the oldest pagoda in Hoi An. Founded in 1454 by a Buddhist monk from China, the main sanctuary shelters a statue of the A Di Da Buddha (Amitabha, the Buddha of the Past), flanked by two Thich Ca Mau Ni Buddhas (Sakyamuni, the Buddha Gautama). **Phuoc Lam Pagoda**, founded in the mid-17th century, is dedicated to the memory of An Thiem, a 17th-century native of Hoi An who became a monk at the age of eight before becoming a soldier and rising to the rank of general. In later years, feeling guilty for all those he had killed, he returned to Hoi An and swept the local market for 20 years to atone for his sins.

Hoi An also retains a number of family chapels. These include the **Tran Family Chapel** on Le Loi Street which was established about two centuries ago as a shrine to venerate the ancestors of the Tran family who moved from China to Vietnam around 1700. The building shows clear signs of Chinese, Japanese and indigenous Vietnamese influence, as does the **Truong Family Chapel** on a nearby side street running south of Phan Chu Trinh Street.

The best-known historical monument in town is **Cau Nhat Ban** or the Japanese Covered Bridge. Built in 1593 by Japanese merchants residing in Hoi An, this ochre-painted wooden bridge crosses a narrow side channel of the Thu Bon River in the western part of town. The bridge has been restored several times but retains a definite Japanese feel. A small temple, **Chua Cau**, is incorporated in the northern side of the bridge.

A related site of interest are the **Japanese Tombs** about 2km (1¼ miles) north of the town centre. The tombstone of the Japanese merchant Yajirobei, who died at Hoi An in 1647, faces northeast towards his homeland and is clearly inscribed with *kanji* characters; a few hundred metres away is the tombstone of another Japanese, Masai by name, who died at Hoi An in 1629. The tombs are difficult, if not impossible, to find without a guide – if you do try, ask the locals for *ma nhat*, the Vietnamese name for the Japanese Tombs.

Temple Statuary

Most Vietnamese temples contain several representations of Buddhas, distinguished by their elongated ear lobes, the presence of an *urna*, or third eye, in the middle of their foreheads, and their tightly curled hair. They are usually represented in one of the classical *mudras*, or attitudes, and seated on a throne, often in the lotus position.

Close by will be statues of the eight Kim Cang, or Genies of the Cardinal Directions, as well as various La Han, or Arhats, and Bo Tat, or Bodhisattvas. These are usually depicted as princes, wearing rich robes and crowns or headdresses. A popular image is that of Quan Cong, usually rosy-cheeked and green-cloaked, accompanied by his two trusty companions, General Chau Xuong and the Mandarin Quan Binh, often with horse and groom.

Hoi An has two other major attractions which make the town a pleasure to visit. The first are the numerous and often very fine **art galleries** which you will find scattered throughout the town, but especially in the area to the east of the Japanese Bridge. Secondly, Hoi An has perhaps the best and most varied collection of **restaurants and cafés** of any town of similar size in Vietnam. Dining in Hoi An is elegant, satisfying and generally very reasonably priced.

The Central Coast

Vietnam's long central coast offers the visitor some of the country's finest beaches and a wide variety of fresh and delicious seafood. It is also rich in history. For over 1,000 years the whole of this beautiful region belonged to the Chams, a seafaring people who built a great Hindu civilisation to the east of the Annamese Cordillera. Over the centuries, as the Vietnamese pressed south, Champa was gradually conquered, forcing many of its citizens to take refuge in nearby Cambodia. Had Champa survived, Indochina would still comprise four countries instead of three, but it was not to be. Today little remains of the lost kingdom other than the brick towers that dot the countryside and scattered communities of ethnic Chams, now a tiny minority in a land they once ruled.

Sorting the catch at Nha Trang

Cham temples follow one basic design. They represent Mt Meru, the Hindu Abode of the Gods, and face East towards the rising sun. The sanctum sanctorum, called *kalan* in Cham, normally had a Shiva *linga* at its centre. Temples usually had three storeys and were undecorated inside. The outer walls of brick and sandstone were carved with considerable skill.

About 40km (25 miles) southwest of Hoi An, beneath the curved peak of **Hon Quap** or Cat's Tooth Mountain, is **My Son**, site of the most significant surviving Cham monuments in Vietnam. My Son was an important religious centre between the 4th and 13th centuries, serving as a spiritual counterpart to the nearby Cham capital at **Tra Kieu**, of which little remains. Traces of around 70 temples and related structures may still be found at My Son, though only about 20 are still in relatively good condition – most of the others were severely damaged by American bombs during the Second Indochina War. My Son is pretty difficult to find, and although it's reached by metalled roads it is best to visit by taxi or minibus, arranged via tour operators in Hoi An or Danang, as the site is well off the beaten track. It's also rather exposed, so in hot, sunny weather be sure to use sunscreen and wear a hat.

At the height of Champa's glory, during the rule of Indravarman IV in the 12th century, the roofs of some of the temples at My Son were reportedly covered with a fine sheath of gold, no sign of which remains today.

The most striking Cham monuments are the famed **Cham Towers**, tall sanctuaries made of bricks joined together in a mysterious fashion that still puzzles the experts, for no bonding material is visible. The best explanation offered to date – though it is still uncertain – is that the Cham master-builders used a form of resin to glue the bricks together. The coast of central Vietnam is studded with Cham Towers from My Son south to Phan Thiet.

Near **Tam Ky**, the capital of Quang Nam Province 62km (39 miles) south of Danang, three towers dating from the 11th century rise from a walled enclosure at **Chien Dang**

Po Nagar: one of Vietnam's most important Cham sites

Cham. Here there are fine sculptures of creatures from Hindu mythology as well as more mundane images of dancers, musicians and elephants. Also near Tam Ky is the important Cham site of **Khuong My**, a temple complex dating from the 10th century which is renowned for the richness of its decorated pillars, pilasters and arches.

About 240km (150 miles) to the south, the restored **Po Nagar Cham Towers** rise on a low hill. This is one of the most important Cham sites in Vietnam, dating back to the 8th century. The temple is dedicated to the goddess Yang Ino Po Nagar and is still venerated by local people, both Viet and Cham.

The Po Nagar towers are about 2km (1¼ miles) north of ➤ **Nha Trang**, an attractive, medium-sized city of about 250,000 people with some of the best beaches in Vietnam. The city has a pleasant, laid-back feel to it and – at least for the present – it remains remarkably untouristed. Nha Trang is a great place to see Cham architecture, soak up the sun and indulge in the freshest of seafood.

It's also one of the best spots in the country for watersports. The waters are clear and clean, and the offshore islands are ideal for snorkelling, scuba diving and fishing. It's easy to hire boats and there are more than 70 islands to explore. The nearest of them, and the most easily accessible by ferry, is **Hon Mieu**. The main attraction here is the **Tri Nguyen**

Aquarium, a pond blocked off from the sea by a dam and divided into three separate sections filled with starfish, turtles, sharks and other marine life. Slightly further out to sea, **Hon Mun** is popular with locals and visitors alike and offers such activities as parasailing, waterskiing, snorkelling, jet-skiing and, of course, sunbathing. The largest island in the small archipelago, **Hon Tre**, is comparatively undeveloped.

Still further south, beyond Cam Ranh Bay – one of the finest natural harbours in Southeast Asia and, in Cold War times, a scene of rivalry between the US and Soviet navies – the twin towns of **Phan Rang** and **Thap Cham** are known chiefly for the excellence of the local grapes. About 7km (4 miles) out of town stands yet another well-preserved and still-venerated Cham monument at **Po Klong Garai**.

The last significant Cham monument in southern Vietnam may be found at **Pan Thiet**, 146km (91 miles) south of Phan

Nha Trang is an attractive town on the estuary of the Cai River

Rang. This quiet coastal city has a large and colourful fishing fleet, best viewed from Tran Hung Dao Bridge in the city centre. The town is also famous for its *nuoc mam* fish sauce. On a low hill to the north of town the 8th-century Cham Towers of **Phu Hai** are worthy of a visit.

Of more significance to most visitors, Pan Thiet is also the gateway to **Mui Ne**, one of the finest beaches in Vietnam and fast developing as a holiday resort, with numerous small hotels. North of town, beyond Phu Hai, a curving white beach stretches for 12km (7½ miles) to Mui Ne fishing village. Along the landward side of the road and, especially, beyond Mui Ne village, there are strange red and white dunes formed from sands that drift in strong winds from the sea.

Dalat and Around

Dalat is Vietnam's premier hill resort. Set by the banks of the Cam Ly River at an altitude of 1,500m (4,875ft), it makes a refreshingly cool change from the heat and humid-ity of the Central Coast and Ho Chi Minh City. Dalat was first established as a hill station at the beginning of the 20th century. It proved popular with the French, and has remained even more so with the Vietnamese.

Dalat's colonial-style cathedral

It's very pleasant to take a stroll around central Dalat, especially in the early evening. The town retains a distinctly Gallic flavour, particularly in the former **French Quarter** around Phan Dinh Phung. Also reminiscent of the colonial era is the pastel pink **Dalat Cathedral** on Tran Phu Road. Completed in 1942, it is dedicated to St Nicolas and has a 47-m (153-ft) high spire and stained glass windows. Popular distractions in the centre of town include **Xuan Hong Lake** and the strangely kitsch **Crazy House**, an organic structure more akin to Modernist creations in Barcelona than anything in Vietnam.

Dalat has numerous pagodas and temples including the **Thien Vuong Pagoda** about 5km (3 miles) southeast of town on Khe Sanh Road. Set on a pine-covered hill, the yellow-coloured pagoda was built by the local Chaozhou community and houses three standing Buddha images made of gilded sandalwood. About 1km (½ mile) southwest of the town centre **Lam Ty Ni Pagoda** was established in 1961 and is set amidst attractive flower gardens. About 1km (½ mile) to the

Writing Vietnamese

The influence of Vietnam's northern neighbour meant that the Vietnamese language was once written in Chinese characters known *chu nho.* All manuscripts and government documents used *chu nho* even after independence in the 10th century. Several tentative attempts were made to modify the Chinese characters, but it was not until the 13th century that the poet Nguyen Thuyen developed a distinct though complex Vietnamese script called *chu nom.* Although standardised for popular literature, *chu nom* never received official recognition, and most Vietnamese scholars continued to use Chinese characters.

A radical change came in the mid-17th century when Alexandre de Rhodes, a French Jesuit missionary, developed a Roman script known as *quoc ngu.* Initially it was used only by the Catholic Church and, after about 1860, the colonial administration. The study of *quoc ngu* became compulsory in secondary schools in 1906, and two years later the royal court in Hue ordered a new curriculum, written entirely in *quoc ngu.* It became the national written language in 1919 and is used throughout the country today.

Traditional weaving in Lang Ga

north of town **Linh Son Pagoda** was established in 1938 and is known for its huge bell, said to be made of bronze mixed with gold.

Dalat was the favoured holiday retreat of Bao Dai, the last of the Nguyen Emperors (1926–45), who enjoyed hunting in the surrounding hills. He ordered the construction of a large villa set amidst pine trees about 2km (1¼ miles) out of town. Completed in 1933, the villa, generally known as **Bao Dai's Summer Palace**, is open to the public. The former imperial living quarters are on the first floor, and here the visitor can see busts of Bao Dai and his father Khai Dinh, together with assorted family pictures.

There are several noted beauty spots around Dalat. **Ho Than Tho**, or the Lake of Sighs, 6km (4 miles) northeast of town, is a popular picnic place surrounded by forested hills. There are several small restaurants near the lake, and it's possible to hire horses to ride in the area. As with Dalat itself, the tourist scene is overwhelmingly Vietnamese, with visitors from Ho Chi Minh City flooding here at weekends.

About 12km (7 miles) northwest of Dalat, at the foot of Lang Bian Mountain, are a group of small settlements which make up **Lat Village**. This is an excellent place to see local hill peoples, still commonly referred to by the French term *Montagnards*. Lat Village is inhabited by people of the Lat minority, as well as by members of related minority groups, the Ma and the Chill. The villagers, who make a living by growing rice, coffee, beans and yams, are known for their pottery and iron-working skills.

The most easily visited minority settlement is **Lang Ga**, conveniently located just off the highway from Dalat to the coast. It is also known as **Chicken Village**, after the large statue of a cockerel that dominates the surrounding houses. The local Koho people are skilled weavers and sell a variety of woven and embroidered goods.

Don Druong, a small town 28km (17 miles) south of Dalat has a large and impressive Cao Dai temple rising on a small bluff to the south of the town. It's not as big as the Cao Dai Holy See at Tay Ninh, but it's just as colourful and the local devotees are pleased to receive visitors.

HO CHI MINH CITY

After reunification in 1975, the Communist authorities extended the municipal boundaries of the former Saigon so that Ho Chi Minh City is now a small province extending from the

A floating market on the Ben Nghe Channel in Ho Chi Minh City

South China Sea almost to the Cambodian frontier. In practice, however, most southerners continue to refer to downtown Ho Chi Minh City as 'Saigon', while the traditional Chinatown area further to the west remains familiarly known as 'Cholon'.

Just as the north is dominated by Hanoi, so the south is dominated by Ho Chi Minh City. Yet here the similarity ends. Where Hanoi is ancient, Ho Chi Minh City is relatively modern. While Hanoi has traditionally been conservative, Ho Chi Minh City is much more go-ahead and willing to embrace new trends and fashions. It is a great city for wining, dining and shopping, but there's much less of historical and cultural interest than in Hanoi.

Downtown Saigon

Central Saigon is almost as much a creation of France as of Vietnam, but the city's rather distinguished colonial style acquired something of an American flavour between 1954

Saigon, the Southern Capital

Three hundred years ago Saigon was no more than a small Khmer fishing settlement called Prey Nokor, a name still widely applied by Cambodian nationalists to the city today. When a group of Chinese refugees from the Qing Empire arrived in the region, the Cambodian governor turned for advice and help to the Nguyen Lords of Hue. The price of settling the Chinese and restoring order was Vietnamese suzerainty. Later the city expanded to join with the nearby Chinese settlement of Cholon – Saigon has always had a strong Chinese flavour to it.

In 1859 the city was seized by France and soon became the capital of the French colony of Cochinchina. Briefly, between 1956 and 1975, Saigon functioned as the capital of the anti-communist Republic of Vietnam. Since the communist seizure of power in 1975, however, it is has once again become overshadowed by its long-term rival Hanoi.

and 1975 when Saigon served as the capital of the US-backed Republic of Vietnam. The Saigonese are a lively people, more intent on doing business and improving their standard of living than on worrying about the past. A good place to start an exploration of the downtown area is the **Song Saigon** or Saigon River. Here one can watch the hustle and bustle of life on the waterfront as small craft jostle for space with larger ocean-going ships and hydrofoils bound for the nearby resort of Vung Tau.

A statue of Ho Chi Minh in the city that now bears his name

Running northwest from the river, **Dong Khoi** – known as Rue Catinat under the French and Tu Do during the American years – is the heart of the former **French Quarter** and leads directly to **Notre Dame Cathedral**, built by the French in 1883. Other distinguished colonial buildings nearby are the splendid **General Post Office** just to the east of the cathedral; the **Municipal Theatre** on Lam Son Square sandwiched between two of Saigon's most distinguished hotels, the **Continental** and the **Caravelle**; and the magnificent former **Town Hall** at the northern end of Nguyen Hue Boulevard.

In the centre of town stands **Dinh Thong Nhat** or Reunification Palace (open daily 7.30–11am, 1–4pm; admission fee), once the official residence of the former Presidents of South Vietnam. Guided tours in English and French will take you from underground war-planning and communications rooms to cavernous banquet rooms and reception halls, to grand sitting and dining rooms, libraries and a theatre. In the grounds stand two T54 tanks of the kind that broke into the former palace in April 1975.

Downtown Saigon isn't noted for its temples, but northwest of the colonial heart of the city, along the broad boulevard named Dien Bien Phu, there are two that are worth visiting. **Chua Ngoc Huang**, or the Pagoda of the Jade Emperor, is at the northern end of Dien Bien Phu near Rach Thi Creek – and, incidentally, by the Dakao Bridge where Graham Greene's fictional Quiet American, Alden Pyle, was found murdered. Built in 1909, this spectacularly colourful Chinese temple is dedicated to Ngoc Huang, the Jade Emperor of the Taoist pantheon. At the junction of Dien Bien Phu and Huyen Than Quan stands **Xa Loi Pagoda**, a Vietnamese temple with murals depicting scenes from the life of the Buddha.

Incense drifts round the Thien Hau Pagoda in Cholon

Right in the heart of Downtown Saigon, **Ben Thanh Market** epitomises the irrepressibly capitalist nature of Ho Chi Minh City. The largest covered market in town, it is packed to overflowing with stalls selling all manner of wares and thousands of busy, haggling shoppers. Most locals will be shopping for fresh food or clothing, but there are also souvenirs for sale – conical *non la* hats, silk *ao dai* costumes, silk-screened T-shirts, coffee from Dalat and a range of imitation antiquities.

The **History Museum** (open Mon–Sat 8–11.30am, 1.30–4.30pm, Sun and holidays 8.30am–4.30pm; free) on Nguyen Binh Kiem houses an impressive collection of artefacts from the Bronze-Age Dong Son culture through the intervening Oc Eo culture to the coming of the Chams, the Khmers and finally the Vietnamese. The exhibits here include a collection of Buddha images from various Asian countries. Art lovers should head for the **Fine Art Museum** (open daily 8–11.30am, 1.30–4.30pm; admission fee) on Pho Duc Chinh. Housed in an attractive yellow and white colonial building, its exhibits include contemporary Vietnamese art, abstract art, Socialist Realism and historic artefacts from Oc Eo, Cambodia and Champa.

Cholon

About 6km (4 miles) west of Saigon lies the bustling city of **Cholon**, Ho Chi Minh City's Chinatown. From the end of the 18th century Overseas Chinese from the coastal provinces of southern China settled in this region, establishing a township physically and ethnically distinct from nearby Saigon. The two have long since merged into a single metropolis, but Cholon retains a distinctly Chinese flavour, especially in and around its temples.

Set in the heart of Cholon, **Nghia An Hoi Quan Pagoda** serves the local Chaozhou community and is chiefly notable for its gilded woodwork. Its shady interior is dominated by huge hanging spirals of incense which burn for up to a month. Just across the road the 19th-century **Tam Son Hoi Quan Pagoda** serves the local Fujian community and is dedicated to Me Sanh, the Goddess of Fertility. Local women come to this faded but richly ornamented temple to pray for children. A short distance to the northwest stands **Thien Hau Pagoda**, built in the early 19th century to serve Cholon's substantial Cantonese community.

North of Cholon by the southern shore of Dam Sen Lake, **Giac Vien Pagoda** is one of the oldest temples in Ho Chi Minh City, founded about two centuries ago. Nguyen Emperor Gia Long is said to have worshipped here. Still further north, in the bleak suburb of Tan Binh, **Giac Lam Pagoda** dates from 1744 and is said to be the oldest temple in the entire Saigon-Cholon region.

DAY TRIPS FROM HO CHI MINH CITY

There are three interesting excursions in the vicinity of Ho Chi Minh City. To the east the seaside resort town of Vung Tau offers sun, swimming and seafood. To the west the claustrophobic tunnels of Cu Chi are a sobering reminder of the Indochina Wars. A short distance further west, Tay Ninh is home to the extraordinary Holy See of the Cao Dai religion.

East of Ho Chi Minh City

The resort town of **Vung Tau** lies at the tip of a triangular peninsula jutting into the sea near the mouth of the Saigon River. It can be reached by minibus or taxi in around 2 hours. En route note the thriving Catholic centre of **Bien Hoa**, with around 15 churches and Christ figures or Madonnas on just about every rooftop. Alternatively – and more relaxingly – hydrofoils leave from the junction of the Saigon River and the Kinh Ben Creek in central Saigon on

Fishing boats in Vung Tau, near the mouth of the Saigon River

a regular basis. The journey takes around 90 minutes and provides a good opportunity to catch glimpses of everyday life in the small riverine fishing villages en route.

Vung Tau or Boat Bay owes its development as a resort to the proximity of Ho Chi Minh City. A resort town that is also partly industrialised, it is home to a major offshore oil company and a large fishing fleet. The beaches are not too bad, but at the same time they are unexceptional by Vietnamese standards. The fresh seafood, on the other hand, is excellent.

West of Ho Chi Minh City

Located about 35km (22 miles) west of Ho Chi Minh City, the district of **Cu Chi** is famous for its extensive underground tunnel network. During the Second Indochina War, the National Liberation Front managed to dig a complex network of underground passages, dormitories, kitchens, munitions factories and hospitals close to Saigon and in spite of

Part of the Cu Chi tunnel network is open to visitors

constant attacks by South Vietnamese and US armed forces. The tunnel network is vast, comprising more than 250km (156 miles) of narrow passageways stretching from the fringes of Ho Chi Minh City to the Cambodian border.

Today two sections of the Cu Chi tunnel network have been renovated and opened to visitors, one at **Ben Dinh** and the other at nearby **Ben Duoc**. A Vietnamese in NLF uniform will guide you to an area of brush or low trees and ask you to locate an entrance to the tunnels. This is far from easy, and few Westerners could pass through the entrance even if they found it. But the enterprising Vietnamese, both proud of their military success at Cu Chi and keen to attract tourists, have enlarged several sections of tunnel to accommodate larger Westerners. The tunnels are still claustrophobic, humid and bat-filled, however, so few visitors will want to stay long underground.

➤ **Tay Ninh**, about 50km (31 miles) beyond Cu Chi and 96km (60 miles) from central Ho Chi Minh City, is the headquarters of Vietnam's – and quite possibly the world's – most idiosyncratic religion. Founded in 1926 by a Vietnamese mystic named Ngo Minh Chieu, Cao Dai or High Tower (a Taoist epithet for God) is a highly syncretic and uniquely Vietnamese philosophy. Cao Dai draws upon traditional Sino-Vietnamese tradition of Confucianism for its moral precepts and Taoism for its occult practices. Buddhism, rooted in Indic tradition but in its Vietnamese variant strongly Sinicised, supplies the doctrines of karma and rebirth. The hierarchical organisation of the church, which includes a pope as supreme patriarch, archbishops and cardinals, is adopted from Roman Catholicism. The same is true for Cao Dai's amazing number of saints. These include Buddha, Confucius, Jesus, Pericles, Julius Caesar, Joan of Arc, Napoleon Bonaparte, William Shakespeare, Victor Hugo and Sun Yat-sen. The Supreme God is represented as an all-seeing eye in a triangle, giving Cao Dai temples something of a cabalistic feel. Worship involves elaborate rituals and festivals.

Within a year of its founding Cao Dai had more than 25,000 followers, and by the 1950s almost 15 percent of all

Black Teeth, White Teeth

Chewing areca nut is an increasingly rare custom in Vietnam. Yet not so long ago, areca nut taken with the leaf of the betel tree and lime paste was consumed throughout the country. Chinese sources from the 6th century describe Vietnam as a region of betel-users, noting that the Chams 'constantly chewed betel', and during the same period Vietnamese fighters, engaged in yet another war with the Chinese, sang a martial song which emphasised this separate identity in the clearest of terms: *Fight to keep our hair long, Fight to keep our teeth black!*

The gradual demise of betel may be traced to the arrival of tobacco, which was first brought to the region in the mid-16th century. Vietnamese men took to tobacco with enthusiasm and betel chewing became increasingly associated with women. Thus, in the mid-19th century ladies of the Vietnamese court at Hue sported their blackened teeth with pride. The emperor informed a priest unwise enough remark on this that 'even a dog can have white teeth'. In Vietnam white teeth, now so highly prized, were once associated with dogs, ghosts – and Europeans.

South Vietnamese were followers. The religion grew in political strength, too. By the end of the First Indochina War in 1954, Tay Ninh Province had become an almost independent Cao Dai fiefdom, where the sect's leadership controlled a private army 25,000 strong. The Cao Dai remained generally aloof from the struggle in the Second Indochina War, and as a consequence suffered considerable persecution following the communist seizure of power in 1975. Today matters are much more relaxed, and it is estimated that there are 3 million followers of Cao Dai in Vietnam, worshipping at more than 400 temples throughout the southern and central provinces, though scarcely any in the north.

Than That Cao Dai or the Great Cao Dai Temple, also commonly referred to as the Holy See, stands 4km (2½ miles) east of Tay Ninh in the village of Long Hoa. Prayers are conducted four times daily at 6am, noon, 6pm and midnight, but visitors should try to attend the noon session as the Cao Dai authorities prefer this and also permit photography. The temple, which rises in nine levels, is richly, some might say gaudily, decorated. Certainly it is surreal, an elaborate pastiche of divine eyes, Cao Dai saints, dragon-swathed pillars and vaulted ceilings. To Graham Greene it was a 'Walt Disney fantasia of the East', while Norman Lewis saw it as 'fun-fair architecture in extreme form'. It is certainly unique and very colourful.

Nui Ba Den, or Black Lady Mountain, is a 986-m (3,204-ft) hill rising out of the rice paddies about 15km (9 miles) northeast of Tay Ninh. Because of its symmetrical shape, and because it stands alone, it has become the recognised symbol of Tay Ninh Province. It's possible to climb Nui Ba Den, visiting a Buddhist temple complex along the way. There are panoramic views of the fertile, rice-growing plains from the summit, and on clear days it's even possible to gaze far into nearby Cambodia. It's also possible to take a cable car to the top of Nui Ba Den.

Worshippers in the extraordinary Great Cao Dai Temple, Tay Ninh

THE MEKONG DELTA

Broad, fertile and criss-crossed by a thousand waterways, the great delta of the Mekong River forms the southernmost part of Vietnam extending to Mui Ca Mau, the cape where the waters of the South China Sea meet those of the Gulf of Thailand. The vast delta region is made up of rich alluvial silt carried down by the floodwaters of the Mekong from neighbouring Cambodia, Laos and Thailand, Burma and China. So regular is this process that the delta is growing at a rate of about 75m (245ft) per year, extending both the shoreline and the rich farmlands of 'Vietnam's Rice Bowl'. A visit to this region enables the traveller to explore shaded waterways and floating markets by boat, see relics of the ancient Funanese city of Oc Eo, and visit Khmer Buddhist temples, Cham Muslim mosques and Hoa Hao temples.

The town of **My Tho** is a sprawling market town by the banks of Cu'a Tien River just 60km (38 miles) southwest of Ho Chi Minh City. After hectic Saigon, My Tho is relatively quiet and a convenient place to explore local waterways and islands. There's not a lot to see in My Tho, although the huge and bustling market provides an interesting insight into delta lifestyles. My Tho's elaborate **Cao Dai Temple** is certainly worth visiting, similarly the pastel-coloured, colonial-period Catholic church and the immaculately-maintained **Vinh Trang** Buddhist Pagoda.

The city of **Vinh Long** is about 60km (38 miles) southwest of My Tho, accessible via an impressive new suspension bridge across the broad Tien Giang, or Upper Mekong River. This is a reasonable overnight stop as there are several adequate hotels and a couple of good restaurants. Vinh Long is famous for the picturesque **Cai Be floating market** about an hour by boat from the city docks. The market functions from around 5am to 5pm, but it's best to visit in the early morning.

Another worthwhile boat trip is to nearby **Anh Binh Island**. Easily reached by small boats that are available for the purpose, the island is very fertile and supports many vegetable gardens and fruit orchards. Boat trips to Cai Be usually stop off at a number of small factories manufacturing local specialities such as spring roll wrappers, rice popcorn, and coconut-based sweets. About 2km (1¼ miles) south of town by the banks of the Rach Long Canal stands **Van Thanh Mieu**, a rather run-down temple dedicated – unusually for the south – to Confucius.

Can Tho, 34km (21 miles) southwest of Vinh Long, is the largest town and *de facto* capital of the Mekong Delta. There's a domestic airport set amidst the myriad waterways, and boat or ferry connections can be made to almost anywhere in the delta. Here, too, the presence of Vietnam's substantial Khmer minority is apparent. **Munirangsyaram**

Vinh Long's picturesque Cai Be floating market

Can Tho makes a good place from which to explore. Accommodation available is the best in the delta and there are several good restaurants.

Pagoda on Hoa Binh Street is the centre of Theravada Buddhism in the city, which has an ethnic Khmer population of around 2,500. There are two interesting floating markets within easy striking distance of Can Tho. These are **Cai Rang**, about 5km (3 miles) southeast of the city, and **Phong Dien**, the most traditional floating market in the delta, situated about 20km (12 miles) southwest of the city.

About 60km (38 miles) northwest of Can Tho, the town of **Long Xuyen** has little to offer, but is a necessary transit point on the way northwest to the Cambodian Frontier. Nearby are the ruins of **Oc Eo**, an important trading port of the Kingdom of Funan which dominated much of the Gulf of Siam coast and the Mekong Delta between the 2nd and 6th centuries. Today little remains of this once great settlement – the passage of time and shifting waters of the Mekong have obliterated all but pottery shards and some pilings. What survives of Funan culture is better viewed at the History Museum and Art Museum in Ho Chi Minh City and the History Museum in Hanoi.

Chau Doc is another delta town, located on the banks of the Hau Fiang or Lower Mekong close by the Cambodian frontier. Until the mid-18th century Chau Doc, like much of the Mekong Delta, was under Cambodian suzerainty. There's still a definite of border atmosphere about the place, and an interesting racial mix. The town is predominantly Vietnamese, but is also home to sizeable Hoa (Chinese), Cham and especially Khmer minorities. The religious mix is still more eclectic. There are Vietnamese and Chinese Mahayana Buddhists, Cambodian Theravada Buddhists, Chinese and Vietnamese Catholics, Cham Muslims, Vietnamese and Khmer Cao Dai and – strangest of all – Hoa Hao, followers of the second major religious sect indigenous to the Mekong Delta.

The Hoa Hao derive their designation from the small village of **Hoa Hao** some 20km (12 miles) east of Chau Doc. An austere and rather ascetic doctrine, Hoa Hao advocates a return to the Theravada ideal of personal salvation combined with aspects of Confucianism and Ancestor Worship. The Hoa Hao movement was born in the 1930s and – like the Cao Dai – soon developed a political philosophy that was both anti-French and anti-Communist. Suppressed in turn by the French, the NLF and (after 1975) by the Communist Government, Hoa Hao still has around 1.5 million followers concentrated mainly around Chau Doc. Hoa Hao men often wear long beards and tie their hair up in a tight bun. Adherents of the sect have their own flag, maroon in colour, and their own special holidays.

Traditional fishing near Ben Tre on the Mekong Delta

37

WHAT TO DO

SHOPPING

Vietnam isn't yet a shopper's paradise, but it seems well on the way to becoming so. During the Second Indochina War, when the US military was present in the south of the country in a big way, just about everything was for sale – much of it 'liberated' from American bases or obtained from the cornucopia of PX stores spawned by the war. Then, in 1975, the victory of the communist north ushered in a new era of austerity and deprivation. Private enterprise was banned, imported goods became an unattainable luxury, and dour, impecunious Russians and East Europeans replaced the hordes of noisy but free-spending GIs. Not surprisingly, the economy fell to previously uncharted depths.

All this began to change following the introduction of *doi moi* economic reforms in 1986. Initially it was a slow process. Most northerners had lived under communism too long to remember anything at all about doing business, and the southerners remained embittered and impoverished. Early visitors to the new Vietnam were pestered by street hawkers and swarms of unfortunate children with little more to offer than postcards and stamps. Fortunately for both Vietnamese merchants and foreign visitors, all this has changed.

Markets and Malls

Prices are generally reasonable in Vietnam. Traditionally, you would be expected to haggle, and this is still the case in markets and backstreet antiques shops – but don't expect huge discounts, as the naturally astute Vietnamese have quickly learned to appreciate real costs and values, even in

Posters and paintings for sale in Hanoi's Old Quarter

Traditional crafts on offer include many smiling Buddhas

once business-shy Hanoi. By contrast, haggling is not expected – or accepted – in obviously fixed-price places such as the new, air-conditioned shopping malls that are beginning to appear in large cities and even smaller towns.

In traditional markets and business districts such as Hanoi's Old Quarter the scent of spices or fish sauce hangs in the air and the sound of haggling is commonplace. As in medieval Europe and the contemporary Middle East, shops selling the same items cluster together in one street and markets have stall after stall specialising in similar goods. You may get a better price by enquiring at each stall and hoping prices fall as the vendors undercut one another. Remember always to smile and be polite – you will get a better price and retain your dignity.

Vietnamese shop for groceries early in the morning. Market shopping tends to be more relaxed in the afternoons when the traders have cooled off a little. In the cities, shopping hours are usually 7.30–11.30am and 1.30–4.30pm, but increasingly shops and malls stay open until 6.30pm or later.

Travellers' cheques and credit cards have made their appearance in Vietnam, but mainly for hotel bills and cash transfers. You will certainly have to use cash to pay for most goods and services, and in most cases Vietnamese dong are preferred to international currencies, though US dollars may also be acceptable.

What to Buy

Traditional Vietnamese handicrafts offer a wide variety of wares to choose from. These include paintings (lacquer, oil, gouache and silk), mother-of-pearl, ceramics, pottery, carved wood, embroidery, bamboo and wickerwork, baskets, sculpture, jewellery, jade (often fake), silks and brocades. You might like to consider adding a *non la*, the ubiquitous Vietnamese conical hat, or an *ao dai*, the traditional costume worn by Vietnamese women, to your wardrobe. Green pith helmets, worn by soldiers during the war and by cyclo drivers and labourers today, are sold in the north, as well as the famous 'Ho Chi Minh sandals' made from used tyre treads. In Ho Chi Minh City toy helicopters, aeroplanes and cyclos made from used cans are cleverly crafted and cheap.

Fake war souvenirs are common – especially 'Zippo' lighters and US army dog tags. There's a big but illicit market in cassette tapes and CDs – everything from traditional Vietnamese music, through Western rock to Cuban and African dance. Enduringly popular and very reasonably priced, T-shirts featuring Vietnamese flags and Socialist Realist

Russian vodka, top-quality caviar and even French champagne may be found at very reasonable prices. Vietnamese coffee is cheap, delicious and makes an excellent souvenir.

designs are available just about everywhere. Clothing is comparatively cheap and local tailors can very quickly produce well-made garments to the design of your choice.

Heavy taxation has discouraged the sale of antiquities, which has remains clandestine and very limited in the north and carefully controlled in the south. Antiques shops in the centre of Ho Chi Minh City and the old quarter of Hanoi sell Vietnamese wood or Laotian bronze Buddhas, old porcelain, ivory carvings, items of silver, small jade statuettes and objects used by the various cults. Increasingly these 'antiques' are clever copies of the real thing, which is good for Vietnam and should satisfy most visitors. Bear in mind that it is forbidden to export certain objects and in principle clearance must be obtained before taking antiquities out of the country.

An unusual and attractive souvenir manufactured mostly in the south and available at Ben Thanh Market is a bamboo screen designed to hang across doorways. Made of hundreds of tiny bamboo cylinders strung on long threads, they are painstakingly painted to show a typical Vietnamese theme – girls dressed in *non la* hats and *ao dai*, for example, or a blossom tree. Considering the work involved, they are very reasonably priced.

Art, both traditional and modern, is widely available

Where to Shop

Hanoi

The Old Quarter – bordered by the railway line and the north side of Hoan Kiem Lake – is filled with little boutiques and stalls overflowing with an astonishing array of goods. Cheap Chinese electronic products,

Colourful handwoven textiles are the speciality of Lang Ga

food, baskets, clothes, Chinese herbal medicines, even marble tombstones. Dong Xuan Market, Hanoi's main covered market, was recently rebuilt after being damaged by fire, and is once again open for business.

Buy silk from shops in Hang Gai Street. Hang Quat Street has red candlesticks and brightly-coloured funeral banners for temple use. Hang Dao stationers have pressed ink blocks, some decorated with gold leaf. You can also find good Chinese paintbrushes for calligraphy or painting. Further south Trang Tien Street is a good area to explore, with some of the best ceramics in town. Red split bamboo plates and bowls make unusual gifts. Down the alleys you will find photocopied and original books and maps, some antique. T-shirts feature political images, such as Ho Chi Minh or Vietnam's national flag (a gold star on a red background).

Vietnam certainly has more art galleries than any other Southeast Asian country. Hanoi is the main centre for this activity, though Ho Chi Minh City and Hoi An are also noteworthy centres for the Fine Arts. Styles vary from traditional Vietnamese painting through Impressionism and Modern Art to Socialist Realism. Galleries in Hanoi can be found around Hoan Kiem Lake, especially to the south and west of the lake.

Hue

Look for the unique 'poem hats' which make an excellent and inexpensive souvenir. In Hue the characteristic *non la* conical hats worn by Vietnamese women everywhere are particularly fine and some may be held up to the light to reveal traditional scenes or poems in silhouette. Also noteworthy are the rice paper and silk paintings. It's best to look for antiques, pseudo-antiques and clothing in the newer part of town, south of the Perfume River. For colourful and traditional markets, head north of the river to the Old City.

Danang and Hoi An

In Danang reasonably priced replicas of Cham statues are available at the Cham Museum souvenir shop. Hoi An is famous for its cotton cloth and silk shops and the small town fairly overflows with clothing boutiques and tailors. If you're looking for tailor-made clothing this is an excellent place to come. Hoi An is in a category of its own where art galleries are concerned, and is emerging as a real cultural gem. Look especially along Tran Phu, especially at the western end in the vicinity of the Japanese Covered Bridge.

Nha Trang

Swimming floats, swimsuits, masks and snorkels are available at the Dam Market. Jewellery and decorations made from shells are found along the esplanade and at Cau Da Port. 'Tortoiseshell' necklaces are really made from turtle shell, though regulations are slowly being enforced to stop this. By contrast the ivory-like material used in jewellery is really fish bone. As elsewhere in Vietnam, there are 24-hour tailor shops and T-shirts for sale, but Nha Trang is a beach resort with few pretensions as a cultural centre.

Hoi An has an astonishing number of art galleries

Dalat

The Central Market in Dalat has a plethora of tourist souvenirs, most of them decidedly kitsch. The three-storey structure (food on the ground floor, souvenirs and clothes on the top two) dates from 1958 and is found at the junction of Nguyen Thi Minh Khai and Le Dai Hanh. Berets, rabbit-skin hats and matching handbags, and curios made of wood and plastic are all found here. In the market square and carried aloft on the backs of street vendors you will find fabrics and basketware made by ethnic minorities as well as fragrant dried teas and excellent Dalat coffee. Try a bottle or two of the reasonably priced Dalat Wine, or *Vang Dalat*. The red is pretty good, but the white might best be described as a cooking wine.

Ho Chi Minh City

This city is a great destination for shoppers. Almost everything, from computer hardware and software, through cameras, imported clothes and pseudo war paraphernalia may be found in the city centre or in Cholon. Dong Khoi and the streets immediately off it have the best souvenir shops. You will find silks, lacquerware and embroideries in abundance. The best place for clothing is the huge Ben Thanh Market. Tailors all over the city are good and many speak English, so take the opportunity to have some clothes made for a fraction the cost you would pay at home – allow 12 to 24 hours for an order to be filled.

Antiques and especially pseudo-antiques abound. Fake antiquities are big business in Vietnam and ceramics and porcelain lead the way. It's probably best to avoid the tourist shops on Dong Khoi Street as prices are high and the bargaining can be tough. Best to head for the Pham Ngu Lao area where there are a number of equally good antiques shops and a somewhat less frenetic atmosphere.

The vast Ben Thanh covered market, the largest in Ho Chi Minh City

NIGHTLIFE

Until 1990 Vietnam had very little nightlife worth speaking of, but since then things have started to change. Before 1975 Saigon was a pretty wild place, with bars, nightclubs and girls on every street corner. All this was swept away by the communist victory, but 15 years of Stalinist orthodoxy didn't change the Saigonese very much, and nowadays Ho Chi Minh City has nightclubs, discos and Karaoke bars aplenty. That said, the Vietnamese authorities still frown upon any nightlife activities that might involve commercial sex, and prostitution – though no doubt existing in Vietnam as it does just about anywhere – is not readily apparent. Vietnam is not yet a serious destination for sex tourism.

Hanoi was always a more staid city than its southern sister, but today the capital is lightening up, though at a slower and more refined pace. Nightlife in Hanoi revolves around wining and dining – there are some very elegant and sophisticated restaurants serving Vietnamese, French and Chinese cuisine – and a developing 'café society'. Elsewhere in the country nightlife is still in its infancy.

Bars and Cafés

At weekends, youth culture in Ho Chi Minh City and Hanoi is on display. Cruising down Ho Chi Minh's fashionable Dong Khoi Street or around Hanoi's Hoan Kiem Lake on a motorcycle and enjoying the more liberal atmosphere is now the done thing for the increasing ranks of middle class youth. Although *bia hoi* establishments exist in other large cities, they are most popular in Hanoi. These small, down-market bars cater exclusively to men – though there would be no objections to a Western woman sitting down for a drink – serving 'fresh beer' without preservatives at amazingly low prices. Vietnamese high society is scarcely likely to visit these bars, but ordinary

Traditional entertainment in Van Mieu, Hanoi

Vietnamese workers such as cyclo-drivers and even teachers may well stop by for a glass on the way home. They can be good places to meet the locals, but usually run out of beer early and close by 8 or 9pm.

Cafés everywhere stay open reasonably late and are filled with couples chatting or just listening to music. Vietnamese generally tend not to drink coffee late at night, and you will probably be offered tea.

Karaoke bars are extremely popular with the Vietnamese. Ballroom dances like the waltz and mambo are still regularly practised at traditional dance halls. There are also increasing numbers of modern discos where locals and visitors dance to the latest international music.

ACTIVE HOLIDAYS

Water sports and diving

With such an extensive coastline Vietnam ought to be a paradise for water sports enthusiasts, but unfortunately for now there are very few organised activities. As Vietnam opens to tourism this should improve. At the moment the best opportunities for scuba diving and snorkelling can be found at Nha Trang, Vietnam's premier beach resort.

Trekking

There are some opportunities for trekking in Vietnam, although at the moment not as many or as sophisticated as in nearby Thailand. Trekking tours can be organised at various travellers' cafés in Hanoi. At present it's probably better not to try to trek in the Central Highlands, as areas around Ban Me Thuot and Pleiku remain politically unstable.

Cycling

A good way to see the country is on a bicycle. Vietnamese roads are by no means the best in the world and sometimes, especially during the rainy season, they can be terrible. While it is theoretically possible to cycle the length of Highway One, from Hanoi to Ho Chi Minh City, it's probably better to be less ambitious and concentrate on cycling in the countryside around Hue or Hoi An and away from the big cities.

Golf

Vietnam may not be the first the place you would think of for a golfing holiday in Asia, but there are some excellent courses. Probably the finest is the International Golf Club of Vietnam

Climbing Fansipan

At 3,143m (10,215ft) Mt Fansipan, Vietnam's highest peak, is only 10km (6 miles) from Sa Pa, but the terrain is difficult and the weather frequently bad. If you are considering scaling the summit, be aware that warm clothes, good boots, camping equipment and a guide are essential, as the round trip may take up to five days. You will also need to carry supplies, so it is best to make arrangements through a local trekking agency. For most of the climb the countryside is completely bereft of signs of humanity – you'll encounter just forest, monkeys, birds and fine mountain views.

in Ho Chi Minh City. In Hanoi try the King's Island Golf Club at Dong Mo Lake some 45km (28 miles) west of the city. At Phan Thiet, 200km (125 miles) north of Ho Chi Minh City, is the challenging Ocean Dunes Golf Club, designed by Nick Faldo, while the hill resort of Dalat has the classy Dalat Palace Golf Club overlooking the majestic Xuan Huong Lake,

ACTIVITIES FOR CHILDREN

On the whole Vietnam is a good destination for families with children. It's not so much that there are numerous and varied activities aimed specifically at children – there aren't. But the Vietnamese are good with children and will pay them a great deal of attention, especially if they are blonde and blue-eyed, in which case they seem as 'doll-like' to the Vietnamese as their sloe-eyed, raven-haired children seem to Europeans and Americans.

There are zoos and amusement parks in both Hanoi and Ho Chi Minh City. The latter, in particular, has a good water park, while in Hanoi the water puppet shows are certain to amuse. Swimming opportunities and water sports are plentiful along the long central coast, though parents should pay attention to safety as facilities for this are very limited.

The Tri Nguyen Aquarium is as colourful as its advertising

Food is not a problem as Vietnamese cuisine is mild beside that of neighbouring Laos, Cambodia and Thailand. Also, the French colonial legacy means familiar dishes from baguette and omelette to steak and *frites* are readily available in most towns and cities.

Calendar of Festivals

Most festivals in Vietnam follow the lunar calendar. In addition to the major nationwide celebrations, there are many smaller local festivals, notably in the Red River Delta where the Viet nation has its origins. Perhaps the best known of all Vietnamese festivals is *Tet*, marked for centuries by the explosion of a million firecrackers. Though these have been banned on grounds of safety, *Tet* is still a pretty noisy occasion as the Vietnamese celebrate with drums – and tape recordings of firecrackers!

January/February: 1st to 7th days of the 1st lunar month: *Tet Nguyen Dan*, or *Tet*, the Lunar New Year. After a tumultuous initial celebration, *Tet* becomes more of a family affair. On the 5th day of the lunar month, *Tay Son*, celebrated in Tay Son district in the Central Highlands, marks the Peasant Rising against the Trinh and Nguyen Lords. On the 5th to 7th days of the month a Water Puppet festival is held at Thay Pagoda west of Hanoi.

February/March: 14 days after *Tet*, at Lill Village, in Bac Ninh Province, *quan ho* songs are performed as men and women sing improvised lyrics of love, compliment and amiable jest.

March: On the 6th day of the 2nd lunar month, the *Hai Ea Trung* festival, at Hai Ba Trung Temple in Hanoi, honours the Trung sisters' resistance to the Chinese.

March/April: At full moon of the 2nd lunar month pilgrims travel to Chua Huong near Hanoi, for the climax of the Perfume Pagoda Festival.

April/May: At Phat Dan lanterns are hung out to celebrate the Buddha's enlightenment on the 8th day of the 4th lunar month.

May/June: 5th day of the 5th lunar month: *Tet Doan Ngo* signals the summer solstice. Celebrations held to ensure good health and well being. The 8th day of the 4th moon is *Dan Sinh* or the Birthday of the Buddha.

August: *Trang Nguyen* marks the Day of Lost Souls on the 14th day of the 7th lunar month. Tombs are cleansed and offerings made to spirits.

September/October: *Kate*, or Cham New Year, at Phan Rang. 14th day of the 8th lunar month, *Trung Thu* or Mid-Autumn Festival is celebrated with dragon dances and gifts of special cakes. Two days later is the Whale Festival at Vung Tau. Crowds gather to make offerings to whales.

EATING OUT

Vietnamese cuisine is among the world's best. It's healthy, being high in fibre and fresh vegetables while low in cholesterol. It's tasty, it's inventive, and it's increasingly based on high-quality ingredients as the country grows more prosperous. Visitors have a wide choice of eating-places – roadside stalls and western-style cafés, government-run canteen-like eateries and Chinese restaurants, hotel restaurants (which are usually good quality) and Vietnamese restaurants serving traditional dishes.

Like so much else in Vietnam, the cuisine reflects long years of cultural exchange with China, Laos, Cambodia and, more recently, France. As elsewhere in Southeast Asia, *com* or rice is the main staple, though bread – especially baguettes introduced by the French – is available everywhere. What's more, bread is always fresh, as it's baked daily. As elsewhere in Southeast Asia, dishes are generally served at the same time rather than by course, and eaten with long-grain rice, dipping sauces and an wide range of fresh herbs and vegetables. Meals are generally eaten with chopsticks or, if European food, with a knife and fork.

Be prepared for locals to throw everything they have finished with, from bones and paper napkins to beer cans, on to the floor beneath the table. This phenomenon is especially noticeable at banquets in small regional eating-houses, though far less so in international restaurants and at popular tourist destinations.

Local Ingredients

Vietnam's long coastline, innumerable rivers, canals and waterways provide an ample and varied supply of fresh fish and seafood all year round. Freshwater and sea fish, shellfish, crabs, octopuses, squids – just about anything that swims or lives in water, including amphibians such as frogs – are eaten as the main source of protein in delicious dishes such as *cha ca*, a barbecued fish made in Hanoi, and in minced fishcakes.

The Vietnamese have created literally hundreds of innovative dishes using pork, chicken and beef, sometimes combining meat together with fish and seafood. Whether boiled, barbecued, grilled, stewed or fried, Vietnamese cuisine skilfully blends numerous flavours, textures and influences. Presentation, too, is important, and a bowl or jug of fresh leaves and herbs set on the table is considered essential.

The fish sauce called *nuoc mam* is ubiquitous in Vietnamese cooking. Set on every table like salt in Western countries or soy sauce in China, *nuoc mam* is used as an ingredient in many dishes, but is also combined with other

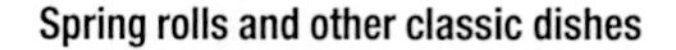

Spring rolls and other classic dishes

Preparing Vietnam-style crab

ingredients as a condiment called *nuoc cham*. The fish sauce has something of a pungent aroma and flavour that can be an acquired taste, but it is a definite complement to the subtle flavours of a cuisine which is, by and large, not too spicy. Manufactured in coastal cities, especially Phan Thiet, the fish sauce is made by fermenting anchovies and salt in large wooden or ceramic vats for about six months.

A dipping sauce is served with starters and a variety of snack-type foods. Every domestic kitchen or restaurant has its own formula, but usually the sauce consists of chilli, lime juice, garlic, sugar and pepper.

Regional Variations

Cuisine varies considerably from one part of Vietnam to another. Generally, food in the north tends to be less spicy, using fewer spices and herbs and – as in neighbouring China – more monosodium glutamate. In the central part of the country around Hue and Danang, food is spicier and also includes creative vegetarian cooking, particularly in Hue, where there are many Buddhists who follow a meatless diet. These vegetarian dishes are often accompanied by, or cooked together with *gao nep*, or glutinous rice – a variety quite distinct from the more familiar long grain types, and closely related to the culinary traditions of neighbouring Laos and northeast Thailand.

Southern cooking, the variety most familiar to those who have eaten in Vietnamese restaurants in America, Australia or Europe, tends to be more flavoursome and varied than that of the north. Often the dishes contain the same ingredients, but they are prepared quite differently.

The south has one essential advantage that helps to explain this: because of the warmer climate there is a much wider variety of fresh fruits and vegetables, including tropical delicacies such as custard apple, sapodilla, durian, pineapple, star fruit, dragon fruit, rambutan and mango. Numerous southern delicacies are served with raw, leafy vegetables, bean sprouts and herbs and wrapped up at table by the diner just before eating. This custom is probably indigenous to the area.

The southerners, living in a tropical area, also use more coconut milk in their cooking and create interesting dishes that combine sweet and sour flavours. The influence of Hoa or Overseas Chinese culinary traditions from Fujian, Hainan and Guangdong is also more apparent in the south, especially in Cholon and throughout the Mekong Delta.

Making rice paper in which spring rolls will be wrapped

Popular Dishes

Some of the more popular Vietnamese dishes include *cha gio* (known as *nem Saigon* in the north): small spring rolls of minced pork, shrimp, crabmeat, fragrant mushrooms and vegetables wrapped in thin rice paper and then deep-fried. *Cha gio* is rolled in a lettuce leaf with fresh mint and other herbs, then dipped in a sweet sauce. *Chao tom* is a northern delicacy: minced shrimp is baked on a stick of sugar cane, then eaten with lettuce, cucumber, coriander *(cilantro)* and mint, and dipped in fish sauce.

Another dish eaten in a similar fashion is *cuon diep*, or shrimp, noodles, mint, coriander and pork wrapped in lettuce leaves. Hue, a city associated with Buddhism, is famous for its vegetarian cuisine and for its *banh khoai*, or 'Hue pancake'. A batter of rice flour and corn is fried with egg to make a pancake, then wrapped around pork or shrimp, onion, bean sprouts and mushrooms. Another Hue speciality is *bun bo*, or fried beef and noodles served with coriander, onion, garlic, cucumber, chilli peppers and tomato paste.

The small but ancient city of Hoi An is also famous for its local specialities. These include *coa lau*, a rice noodle soup

Dine afloat in this floating restaurant on West Lake, Hanoi

said to be based on the Japanese *soba* tradition, served with slices of lean pork, soy sauce and fresh lime juice. This is usually topped with crumbled *banh da* or rice crackers. Other local Hoi An specialities include fried *won ton* dumplings – perhaps, like the *soba*-based noodles, a legacy of the port's multicultural past – and the enduringly popular 'white rose', or steamed shrimps wrapped in rice paper.

Soups for All Seasons

Soups are popular throughout the country, and generally served with almost every meal. *Mien ga* is a noodle soup, most popular in the south, blending chicken, coriander, fish sauce and scallions. *Hu tieu* is chicken, beef, pork and shrimp served with a broth over rice noodles mixed with crabmeat, peanuts, onion and garlic. *Canh chua*, a sour soup served with shrimp or fish head, is a fragrant blend of tomato, pineapple, star fruit, bean sprouts, fried onion, bamboo shoots, coriander and cinnamon.

But undoubtedly the best known of all Vietnamese soup dishes, often eaten for breakfast or as a late night snack, is *pho*, a broth of rice noodles topped with beef or chicken, fresh herbs and onion. Egg yolk is often added, as may be lime juice, chilli peppers or vinegar. *Pho* is generally served with *quay* – a fried piece of flour dough. Northerners often say that southern *pho* is too sweet, while southerners claim the northern variant is too bland – yet both agree that *pho* is indeed a veritable staff of life.

Another type of noodle dish, mostly popular in the south, is *mien ga* – a soup of chicken, coriander, fish sauce and spring onions. *Canh chua* is a sour soup generally served with shrimp or fish head; the stock is a fragrant blend of sweet and tangy flavours, using tomato, pineapple, star fruit, bean sprouts, fried onion, bamboo shoots, coriander, cinnamon and, naturally, *nuoc mam*.

Exquisitely carved vegetables decorate these duck and beef dishes

Other delicious dishes which exemplify Vietnamese cooking include *cha lua* – pork paté wrapped in banana leaves before cooking and served in baguettes as a popular streetside snack – and *chao tom*, a delicious and popular Hanoi speciality made from minced shrimp baked on sugar cane. The shrimp is removed from the sugar cane and rolled in rice paper with lettuce, cucumber, coriander and mint, and dipped in *nuoc cham* sauce.

Cuon diep is shrimp, noodles, mint, coriander and pork wrapped in lettuce leaves – particularly good in Nha Trang. Available just about everywhere, *goi ga* is shredded chicken marinated in onion, vinegar, mint and, sometimes, peanuts – best eaten with white, long-grain rice. *Ga xao sa o* is sautéed chicken cooked with lemongrass, fish sauce, garlic, onion and chillies. Sometimes peanuts are added.

Bun bo is a Hue speciality consisting of stir-fried beef, served over noodles with coriander, onion, garlic, cucumber, chillies and tomato paste. Popular in the south, *hu tieu* is a tasty mix of chicken, beef, pork and shrimp served with a broth over rice noodles, with crab meat, peanuts, onion and garlic. *Banh cuon* is a steamed rice pancake rolled around minced pork. Enduringly popular and closely associated with Hue, *banh khoai* is a kind of omelette made from a batter of rice flour and cornstarch which is fried with egg and wrapped around pork or shrimp, onion, bean sprouts and mushrooms.

What to Drink

Bottled fresh water, canned and bottled soft drinks and canned beers are available throughout the country. The range of beers, in particular, is extensive, with most large cities having at least one brand of their own. Unfortunately nearly all are tinned, though bottled beers are making an appearance, especially in Hanoi and Ho Chi Min City. Most beers are rather light and unremarkable, and draught beer remains a rarity. An unusual Vietnamese institution is *bia hoi*, or 'fresh beer', a concept first introduced by the Czechs but now beloved of beer-drinkers all over the country. Beer without preservatives is delivered fresh daily in small tanker-trucks. *Bia hoi* establishments are usually very basic, but they are good places to meet the locals and the price is extraordinarily low – somewhere around 2,200 Dong or US15 cents for a large glass.

French and Australian wines are increasingly popular, especially at restaurants in Hanoi, Ho Chi Minh City and other large cities. Locally produced wine is also available, made from

As a legacy of Vietnam's recent history, Stolychnaya and other Russian vodkas may be found on some shelves, but these are rapidly being replaced by locally-produced vodka.

grapes grown at the extensive vineyards near Phan Thiet and Phan Rang and bottled in Dalat. Vang Dalat (the name is an approximation of the French *vin*) is reasonably priced and the red, at least, is not at all bad. The white is another matter, and is just about quaffable if served very cold. Local rice liquors are cheap and fierce.

A wide variety of fresh fruit juices and juice shakes are available. One unusual variant, only just making its debut in the markets and delicatessens of the West, is dragon fruit – a magenta-coloured fruit whose white flesh is speckled with black seeds. All over the country, especially in the centre and the south, are *sinh to* stalls, easily recognised by their glass cases displaying a variety of colourful fruits and vegetables. Point to a selection of fruit and you will receive a liquidised fruit-and-ice shake, prepared with or without sugar *(duong)* as you prefer.

Try the Dalat-made 'Vang'

Chinese tea, served both hot and cold, is served everywhere. Vietnamese coffee, grown in the Central Highlands and served with tiny individual metal filters, is simply delicious.

International cuisine

Vietnamese food is a delight, and aficionados rank it right up there with such great schools of Asian cuisine as Chinese, Thai,

Japanese and Indian. Still, if you desire something more familiar there should be no problem in any but the most remote of destinations. In recent years there has been something of an explosion of bistro and pub-style restaurants in Hanoi and Ho Chi Minh City. Good international food is available in most towns, and new French, Italian, Chinese, Thai and Japanese restaurants are opening on an almost weekly basis. There's good Indian food, too – look in particular for the small but excellent chain of Omar Khayyam restaurants to be found in Hanoi, Hue, Danang and Saigon. Some of the best French cuisine in the country may be had in the hill station of Dalat.

To help you order...

Restaurant	**Nha hang**
Do you have an English menu?	**Ban co thuc don ban tieng Anh khong?**
Not too spicy, please	**Xin dung cho cay qua**
I'm a vegetarian	**Toi an chay**
I'd like something to drink	**Xin cho phan giai khat**
Can I have a beer, please?	**Cho toi xin chai bia?**
Please may I have the bill	**Xin tinh tien**

and read the menu...

com	rice	**com chien**	fried rice
banh mi	bread	**ga**	chicken
thit heo	pork	**thit bo**	beef
vit	duck	**ca**	fish
tom to	prawn	**con muc**	squid
trung	egg	**rau song**	vegetables
tra	tea	**ca phe**	coffee
nuoc cat	water (distilled or bottled)		

HANDY TRAVEL TIPS

An A–Z Summary of Practical Information

A

ACCOMMODATION

The standard of Vietnamese accommodation has come a long way in the last few years, and you will find international standard hotels in most of the larger cities. Ho Chi Minh City offers the widest range of top quality hotels, but Hanoi is catching up fast. Outside of these cities, five-star hotels are certainly harder to find, but new hotels are opening all the time. Most hotel rooms in the big cities now offer satellite television and sometimes even a computer with Internet access. Beach resorts such as Nha Trang and Mui Ne offer a wide variety of accommodation to suit all pockets.

Generally the number of rooms available at any time far outstrips the demand – with the notable exception of Hoi An, though this popular destination is building new hotels fast. This is worth remembering when you come to check on rates: it is possible to bargain.

Hotel	**khach san**
Guesthouse	**nha khach**
I'd like a single/double room with bathroom	**toi muon mot phong chiec/doi phong tam**
What's the rate per night?	**moi dem bao nhieu?**

AIRPORTS

Vietnam has three international airports, Hanoi's Noi Bai airport, Ho Chi Minh City's Tan Son Nhat and Danang International Airport.

Tan Son Nhat, the busiest of the three, is located 7km (4 miles) or 15 minutes northeast of downtown Ho Chi Minh City. Metered taxis are available and far better organised than in Hanoi. Fares start at about 60,000 dong (US$4).

Noi Bai airport is 35km (22 miles) north of Hanoi. Vietnam Airlines provides a shuttle bus service to and from Pho Quang Trung, the central Hanoi booking office, for US$4 per person. Taxis are available in front of the terminal building and a typical fare to anywhere in downtown Hanoi would be US$10.

Danang International Airport is 2km (1 mile) west of the town and has been developed as a regional airline entry point.

A departure tax of US$12 is levied for all international flights and can be paid in either dong or dollars. Domestic departure tax is now included in the ticket price.

B

BICYCLE AND MOTORBIKE HIRE (RENTAL)

For most Vietnamese, bicycles still provide the main means of transport. For the visitor they are a great way to see Vietnam. Bicycles can be hired from various cafés, travel agents and hotels in Hanoi and Ho Chi Minh City. For the Imperial City of Hue a bicycle is the perfect way to see the sights. In recent years more and more cyclists have taken to touring the country on mountain bikes. Most buses and trains will allow bicycles on board and there are bicycle repair shops in most towns.

Motorbike hire is possible in most cities and resorts, from some cafés, travel agents and hotels, but for getting around the big cities it's only a good idea if you have some previous experience. The traffic in Hanoi is overwhelming, though slow, and does not appear to follow any road rules. In Ho Chi Minh City, the streets are wider and things move at a much quicker pace, so great care is needed. Visitors are not allowed to drive any motorbike over 125cc. The usual cost of a day's motorbike hire should be US$4–5.

Where can I hire a bicycle?	**Toi co the muon xe dap o dau?**
Where can I hire a motorbike?	**Toi co the muon xe mo to o dau?**

BUDGETING FOR YOUR TRIP

Hanoi and Ho Chi Minh City are not expensive when compared with other major cities of the world.

Transport. Taxi: 8,000–25,000 dong (US50c–$1.50)
Cyclo: 5,000–10,000 dong (US30–70c)
Average fare of a domestic one-way flight (Hanoi to Ho Chi Minh City): 1,800,000 dong (US$112)
Average fare of a domestic rail ticket (Ho Chi Minh City to Nha Trang): 167,000 dong (US$10)
Average fare of a domestic bus ticket (Ho Chi Minh City to Hue): 100,000 dong (US$6)

Meals. Dining at luxury hotels is considerably more expensive than at a local restaurant. On average, breakfast and lunch will cost around 35,000 dong (US$2), although a bowl of noodles on the street can cost as little as 8,000 dong (US 50 cents). More upmarket restaurants serve main courses starting at around 45,000 dong (US$3). Expect a top-class dinner to be at least US$10 per person.

C

CAMPING

At the moment there is little provision for individuals wanting to camp, but a few travel agents (Sinh Café Travel, Hanoi; tel: (844 934 4103) do offer camping trips into the Central Highlands and around Halong Bay.

CAR HIRE (RENTAL)

The rules on car rental have been relaxed recently and it is now possible to drive yourself, but because of the extreme chaos on the roads and the state of many highways it is advisable to hire a car with a driver. There are advantages to this: the driver will stay with the car to protect both the vehicle and your belongings, sometimes even to the extent of sleeping in the car at night. You can hire cars from hotels and travel agents from US$25–60 per day, depending on the make and model.

One very convenient way to see the country is to hire a car and driver in Hanoi or Ho Chi Minh and drive the length of Highway One which connects the two major cities. This can take as long as you like, but it's best to allow a week to ten days, stopping at Mui Ne, Dalat, Nha Trang, Hoi An and Hue en route. This option will cost around US$500–600.

Where can I hire a car?	**Toi co the muon xe hoi o dau?**
How much is the daily rate?	**Gia bao nhieu tien mot ngay?**
How much is the weekly rate?	**Gia bao nhieu tien mot tuan?**
Is insurance included?	**Co bao gom bao hiem?**

CLIMATE

Due to its location in the Southeast Asian monsoon zone, stretching over 14 degrees from north to south, Vietnam's climate varies from region to region. The climate in the north is influenced by the winds of Central Asia and from November to April northern Vietnam experiences a relatively cool and humid winter. In the mountains temperatures fall as low as freezing point. Between May and October, temperatures rise, coupled with heavy rain and sometimes typhoons. Both the north and centre's hottest months are June, July and August.

Southern Vietnam's climate is characterised by relatively constant temperatures, a season of heavy rains between May and October, a relatively dry season from November to February, and a hot season between February and April when temperatures may reach 35°C (95°F). The rains are usually heavy and conditions during this period can be sticky and uncomfortable.

Hanoi is generally cooler than Ho Chi Minh City and is prone to greater temperature extremes (8–33°C/46–91°F). Ho Chi Minh

City is hot most of the year (21–36°C/70–97°F). The Hai Van Pass just north of Danang acts as a climatic barrier between north and south. Hue and Danang may be only about 3 hours' drive apart, but the former is decidedly colder, especially in winter.

CLOTHING

As Vietnam is a mainly Buddhist country you'll find yourself removing your shoes on a regular basis, be it in a temple or visiting someone's home, so bring shoes that are easily removable. In the cool season months the north of the country, especially in the mountains around Sa Pa, can be quite cold, so pack a sweater. At certain times the sun can be very fierce so a sun hat is a good idea. Generally loose cotton clothes are recommended, and waterproof footwear for the rainy season. It's also a good idea to keep a cheap plastic raincoat in your travelling bag.

On the whole Vietnam is a relaxed country when it comes to dress, although monks prefer people not to wear T-shirts and shorts when visiting temples and other holy sites.

CRIME AND SAFETY

Compared to many countries Vietnam is a remarkably safe place to visit and you are unlikely to have serious problems. Pickpockets can be a problem in Ho Chi Minh City, especially around the tourist areas. Be especially aware of groups of children selling postcards and pressing in on you when trying to sell to you. Obviously the majority are not trying to steal from you, but do be careful. It's also best not to wear jewellery that can be easily snatched. When walking or travelling in a cyclo, keep one hand firmly on your handbag or camera.

If you are travelling on long-distance buses be aware of overly friendly people offering you free drinks: the drinks can be drugged. When you wake up some hours later your valuables will have been removed, and the thief will have left the bus.

I want to report a theft	**Chung toi muon bao cao mot vu pham phap**
My handbag/wallet/ticket has been stolen	**Xach tay/Vi tien/Ve cua toi da bi an cap**
My passport has been stolen	**So thong hanh cua toi da bi an cap**
Help! Thief!	**Cuu toi! An cap!**

CUSTOMS AND ENTRY REQUIREMENTS

A visa is essential for Vietnam. The length of time it takes to get a visa varies depending on where you apply for it, but usually a single entry 30-day tourist visa can be processed in five working days and costs around US$40. The Vietnamese embassy in Bangkok has a good reputation and usually only takes four days. Visas can be extended once for 30 days at a cost of about US$30. Extensions are best processed by a local travel agent in either Ho Chi Minh City or Hanoi. Always make sure your passport is valid for at least another 6 months.

Duty-free allowances per person are 2 litres of liquor, 200 cigarettes, and 50 cigars or 250g of tobacco. It is a good idea to keep a list of expensive items you bring in to the country as you may be questioned about them when you leave. Restrictions include non-prescription drugs, pornography, firearms, and certain fruits and vegetables.

I have nothing to declare	**Toi khong co gi de khai bao**

D

DRIVING

Vietnamese drive on the right. Unfortunately the standard of driving in Vietnam leaves a lot to be desired and cars and trucks often drive on the wrong side of the road. Both Hanoi's and Ho Chi Minh City's roads are clogged with traffic and driving yourself is a hazardous undertaking. An excessive use of the horn is all too common.

Stop	**ngung**
Slow down	**chay cham lai**
No entry	**cam vao**
No parking	**cam dau**
One way	**mot chieu**
Danger	**nguy hiem**
Pedestrian	**nguoi di bo**
Speed limit	**to do gioi han**
Turn left/right	**queo sang trai / sang phai**
Fill the tank, please	**Lam on do day bing**
Petrol	**dau**
Leaded	**co chat chi**
Unleaded	**khong co chi**

E

ELECTRICITY

Electricity is rated at 220 volts, although you may still find the odd place rated at 110 volts. Sockets are of the standard European or American type (two-pin; both round and flat prongs are equally common).

EMBASSIES/CONSULATES

Embassies in Hanoi:

Australia: 8 Dao Tan; tel: (04) 831 7755; fax: 831 7711.

Canada: 31 Hung Vuong Street; tel: (04) 823 5500; fax: 823 5333.

New Zealand:, 63 Ly Thai To; tel: (04) 824 1481; fax: 824 1480.

South Africa: 59A Ly Thai To; tel: (04) 934 0888.
United Kingdom: Central Building, 31 Hai Ba Trung Street; tel: (04) 936 0500; fax: 936 0561.
United States: 7 Lang Ha Street; tel: (04) 772 1500; fax: 772 1510.

Consulates in Ho Chi Minh City:
Australia: 5b Ton Duc Thang Street, District 1; tel: (08) 829 6035; fax: 829 6031.
Canada: 235 Dong Khoi Street, District 1; tel: (08) 824 5025; fax: 829 4528.
United Kingdom: 25 Le Duan Street, District 1; tel: (08) 823 2604; fax: 829 5257.
United States: 4 Le Duan Street, District 1; tel: (08) 822 9433; fax: 822 9434.

EMERGENCIES

For all emergencies in Vietnam ring 116. Other numbers include 113 (Police) and 114 (Fire). For directory enquiries ring 116.

G

GAY AND LESBIAN TRAVELLERS

On the whole homosexuality is tolerated in Vietnam, although it is best not to flaunt it. The gay scene is in evidence most notably in Hanoi and Ho Chi Minh City where there's an active café society.

GETTING TO VIETNAM

By Air There are a number of ways to reach Vietnam, but the usual, and easiest, is by air. Because of the variety of fares available it is best to contact an experienced travel agent before leaving home. Some of the cheaper air tickets need to be booked well in advance. Look for the best deals in the weekend newspapers.

A number of international airlines fly to Vietnam with direct daily flights from Bangkok, Hong Kong, Kuala Lumpur, Phnom Penh and Singapore. Other direct flights to Hanoi's Noi Bai airport include Dubai, Guangzhou, Kunming, Moscow, Paris, Seoul, Taipei, Tokyo and Vientiane. Ho Chi Minh City's Tan Son Nhat airport has direct links with Dubai, Manila, Melbourne, Osaka, Paris, Seoul, Siem Reap, Sydney, and Taipei. It is advisable to reconfirm all your flights 72 hours before take off.

By Road It's possible to enter Vietnam by land at a number of border crossings. From Cambodia there are three crossing points: Chau Doc, Vinh Xuong and Moc Bai. From Laos: Lao Bao and Cau Treo. From China: Lao Cai, Dong Dang and Mong Cai.

By River It's now possible to enter Vietnam by riverboat from Cambodia. Ferries leave Phnom Penh via the Bassac River or Lower Mekong (which becomes the Song Hau Giang in Vietnam). The border entry point is at Chau Doc in the Mekong Delta.

GUIDES AND TOURS

A number of excellent travel agencies operate in Hanoi and Ho Chi Minh City offering tours and guides to all parts of the country. Of particular use are:

Buffalo Tours, 11 Pho Hang Muoi Street, Hanoi; tel: (04) 828 0702; <www.buffalotours.com>. Very good for adventure tours and trips into the mountainous north.

SinhBalo Adventures, 283/20 Pham Ngu Lao, District 1, Ho Chi Minh City; tel: (08) 837 6766; <www.sinhbalo.com>. This was set up by Le Van Sinh, one of Vietnam's original tour operators and owner of the famed Sinh Café.

Vietnam Europe, 40 Truong Quyen Street, District 3, Ho Chi Minh City; tel: (08) 820 2563; <www.vietnameurope.com>. They have close links with a number of European tour operators.

H

HEALTH AND MEDICAL CARE

Immunisation is recommended against cholera, typhoid, tetanus and hepatitis.

Always drink bottled water, which is widely available, never tap water. Avoid eating raw vegetables and fruit without thoroughly washing and peeling them yourself.

Malarial mosquitoes are widespread in the countryside, but as long as you are staying close to the tourist areas there should be no real problems. Nevertheless it is advisable to bring along some good mosquito repellent for use on exposed skin at night. After dark it is advisable to wear long sleeved-shirts and long trousers. Be especially careful in the west of the Central Highlands along the Cambodian frontier. Consult your doctor about any recent advances in the treatment of malaria.

For medical attention in Hanoi, try the 24-hour **International SOS Hospital**, 31 Hai Ba Trung Street; tel: (04) 934 0555.

In Ho Chi Minh City try the **International Medical Centre**, 1 Han Thuyen Street, District 1; tel: (08) 827 2366.

Where is a chemist?	**Hoa hoc gia o dau?**
Where is a doctor?	**Bac si o dau?**
Where is a dentist?	**Nha so o dau?**
Sunburn/sunstroke	**Chay nang**
An upset stomach	**Dau bung**

HOLIDAYS

Many of Vietnam's major holidays are tied to the lunar calendar and therefore vary from year to year. There are however a number of official public holidays on fixed dates:

1 January New Year's Day

3 February Communist Party of Vietnam Day

30 April Liberation of Saigon
1 May International Labour Day
19 May Ho Chi Minh's Birthday
27 July War Martyrs' Memorial Day
2 September National Day
25 December Christmas Day
Moveable Dates

All the following celebrations are lunar festivals:

January/February: *Tet Nguyen Dan* (Vietnamese Lunar New Year) or Tet for short is the most important festival of the year. Many Vietnamese take a whole week off for their celebrations, but officially the festival lasts three days. It usually falls between January and February.

January/February: *Dong Da* Day celebrates Vietnam's victory over the Chinese in 1789.

March/April: *Thanh Minh* (Holiday of the Dead) honours the dead. Families make trips to the graves of deceased relatives.

April/May: *Phat Dan* celebrates the Buddha's Birth, Enlightenment and Death. Buddhists visit temples, shrines and private homes.

June/July: *Trung Nguyen* (Wandering Soul's Day) is the second most important festival of the year. Offerings are made to the wandering souls of the dead.

November/December: Confucius' Birthday.

For more details of religious festivals, *see page 99*.

L

LANGUAGE

Vietnamese is spoken by virtually the entire population and is a fusion of Mon-Khmer, Tai and Chinese elements. A significant proportion of its base vocabulary is derived from Mon-Khmer, a non-tonal language group. Today's Vietnamese is tonal and this has been acquired over the centuries mainly from neighbouring

Tai-speaking peoples. The Chinese element, which is also tonal, consists of an extensive vocabulary, especially in the realms of philosophy, literature and administration.

Vietnamese is not an easy language to master and requires intensive study, but it is possible to learn some basic vocabulary and this will be much appreciated by the locals. Particularly useful are numbers, food and travel terms. With Vietnam's burgeoning tourist industry more and more young people are learning English and are only too pleased to get in some practice. If you are fortunate enough to speak French you will find a number of older people, especially in urban areas, still able to communicate in the old colonial language. Chinese is understood by many Vietnamese of Chinese descent, especially in Cholon.

Monday	**thu hai**	Friday	**thu sau**
Tuesday	**thu ba**	Saturday	**thu bay**
Wednesday	**thu tu**	Sunday	**thu nhat**
Thursday	**thu nam**		
one	**mot**	eleven	**muoi mot**
two	**hai**	twelve	**muoi hai**
three	**ba**	thirteen	**muoi ba**
four	**bon**	fourteen	**muoi bon**
five	**nam**	twenty	**hai muoi**
six	**sau**	twenty-one	**hai muoi mot**
seven	**bay**	twenty-two	**hai muoi hai**
eight	**tam**	thirty	**ba muoi**
nine	**chin**	fifty	**nam muoi**
ten	**muoi**	ninety	**chin muoi**
100	**mot tram**	10,000	**muoi nghin**
200	**hai tram**	100,000	**tram nghin**
1,000	**mot nghin**	1,000,000	**mot trieu**

M

MAPS

Many travel agents and hotels have quite basic locally produced town maps, but unfortunately they rarely extend beyond the town or province. One excellent map that is available in most good international bookstores is the *Insight Travel Map: Thailand, Vietnam, Laos, Burma & Malaysia* (1:4,000,000).

MEDIA

At 11pm every night, Vietnam television on Channel 9 gives the news headlines in English, and at major hotels, BBC World Service or CNN are generally available. The best local English-language newspapers are the daily *Vietnam News* and weekly *Vietnam Investment Review*, and magazines like the monthly *Vietnam Economic Times* and *Vietnam Today*. These are targeted at foreign investors and their main purpose is to emphasise local investment opportunities. There are no local radio stations that broadcast in English, but you can tune in to the BBC World Service or the Voice of America.

MONEY

The unit of currency in Vietnam is called the dong, abbreviated *d* (1US$ = 16,000 dong). Banknotes come in denominations of 200*d*, 500*d*, 1,000*d*, 2,000*d*, 5,000*d*, 10,000*d*, 20,000*d*, 50,000*d* and 100,000*d*. US dollars are widely accepted at the airports, in hotels and sometimes taxi drivers will take them. Room rates are often quoted in dollars in the better hotels.

Theoretically most major currencies can be exchanged in Vietnam, but in reality it is better to bring US dollars. At the moment only certain travellers' cheques and credit cards are acceptable in the big cities. Cheques and cards accepted include Visa, MasterCard and American Express. The most organised bank for exchanging travellers' cheques and money is the state-owned Vietcombank.

Where is a bank?	**Nha bang o dau?**
I want to change...	**Toi muon doi...**
some money	**tien mat**
travellers' cheques	**chi phieu du lich**
Can I pay with a credit card?	**Ban co nhan the tin dung khong?**

O

OPENING HOURS

Government offices and the offices of official bodies are usually open Mon–Fri 8am–11.30am and 2pm–5pm, Sat 8am–noon. Museums are usually open Tues–Sun 8am–12am and 2pm–5pm, but it is advisable to check individual museums before planning a visit. Temples are generally open daily 6am–6pm.

Shops and supermarkets are mostly open daily from as early as 6am and close any time from 6–10pm. Banks are open Mon–Fri 8am–3pm, Sat 8am– noon. Post offices are generally open every day 6am–8pm. Banks, administrative offices and museums, but not post offices, are closed on all public holidays and occasionally on religious festivals.

Vietnam works a six-day week, with Sunday as the rest day. Business hours are from 7.30–11.30am and 2–4.30pm. The lunch hour can vary, but very rarely do banks and shops stay open at this time. You'll find the lunchtime siesta period more noticeable in the centre and the south, and some towns, such as Danang, can be extremely quiet.

P

POLICE

Noted for their rather bright olive green uniforms, the police in Vietnam are not known for their friendly manner or their knowledge of the English language. So if you do get something stolen and need a report for your insurance company, it's best to take an English-speaking Vietnamese along with you to the police station. The emergency police number is 113. In dealing with the police it's always best to smile and be polite: losing your temper will only make the situation worse. Traffic police wear brown rather than green uniforms.

POST OFFICES

Post offices are found in most towns and many have facilities for faxes and express mail services. The quickest services out of the country are from the larger cities. The main post office in Hanoi is Buu Dien Ha Noi, 75 Dinh Tien Hoang Street (tel: 825 4413; fax: 825 0000); in Ho Chi Minh City, it's the Buu Dien Ho Chi Minh, next to Notre Dame Cathedral (tel: 829 9446; fax: 829 8540). These post offices will keep faxes that you can redeem for a small fee. Faxes can also be sent from most major hotels in Ho Chi Minh City and Hanoi. Post offices offer two quick registered mail services called EMS and PCN.

PUBLIC TRANSPORT

Taxis

All the large towns have taxi services and all vehicles are metered. Sometimes it is easier to ring the company than wait on the street for a taxi to turn up. In Hanoi try Airport Taxis (tel: 873 3333), Hanoi Taxis (tel: 853 5252) or Mai Linh Taxis (tel: 822 2666). For Ho Chi Minh City try Airport Taxis (tel: 844 6666), Mai Linh Taxis (tel: 822 2666) or Vina Taxis (tel: 811 0888).

Long-distance taxis

One of the best ways of getting around in Vietnam, though definitely not the cheapest, is by long-distance taxi. These can easily be arranged by your hotel or at a local tour agency. You can either hire a car and driver by the day, moving on from town to town, or engage a driver for a longer period – for example 10 days or so which allows adequate time to drive from Hanoi to Ho Chi Minh City and see all the principal sights along the way. Driving standards are generally acceptable (cars are expensive in Vietnam and their owners do their best to look after them). An air-conditioned car and driver costs between US$40 and US$60 a day, depending on the distance travelled. If you are a keen photographer, then this has to be the means of transport of choice, as you can ask the driver to stop whenever and wherever you want.

Cyclo

Though quite slow the cyclo, or trishaw, is a great way to get around most towns. If you have time on your hands there is no better way to see the sights. Many drivers, especially in Ho Chi Minh City, speak some English. Cyclos are banned from some of the larger streets in Hanoi and Ho Chi Minh City and the driver will have to make certain detours.

Bus

Vietnam has an extensive bus network, but travelling this way can be tiring and even quite dangerous. Roads in Vietnam are not yet up to the standards found in other Southeast Asian countries. Large express buses travel between most of the major towns and cities. Unfortunately buses do tend to be overcrowded and prone to frequent breakdowns. If you have to travel by bus it is best to make the journey in daylight hours as many vehicles travel without lights at night.

Train

Vietnam's rather aged rail network stretches between Hanoi and Ho Chi Minh City. It is served daily by the Reunification Express that stops at many towns on the way. The journey between the two cities usually takes between 36 and 44 gruelling hours. It is a safer way to travel than the bus, but be careful about leaving your belongings unattended, it's a good idea to bring a padlock with you. Food is available on the trains and a variety of snack vendors will come aboard at sations. Air-conditioned sleepers are available and make the trip between Hanoi and Ho Chi Minh City a more bearable experience. From Hanoi there are rail links to the Chinese border at Lao Cai and Lang Son, and also to the port city of Haiphong. It is advisable to book well ahead as trains are often full. For a sleeping berth you may need to book as much as four days in advance. Travel agencies and hotels can help arrange tickets, so you will not necessarily have to go to the railway booking offices. For further information on Vietnam's rail network go to the website <www.vr.com.vn/English>.

In Hanoi, the train station is at 120 Le Duan Street; tel: 942 3697. In Ho Chi Minh City, go to 1 Nguyen Thong Street; tel: 843 6528.

Where is the bus stop?	**Tram xe buyt o dau?**
Where is the railway station?	**Ga xe lua o dau?**
When is the next bus for...?	**May gio thi chuyen xe buyt... se toi?**
When is the next train for...?	**May gio thi chuyen tau lua ... se toi?**
I want a ticket to...	**Toi muon dat truoc mot ve di...**
single (one-way)	**Ve di mot chieu**
return (round trip)	**Ve khu hoi**
Will you tell me when we get to...?	**Khi xe den ... ban co the bao ch o toi biet khong a?**

R

RELIGION

Most Vietnamese would describe themselves as Buddhists, but theirs is a very different Buddhism from that practised elsewhere in mainland Southeast Asia. Buddhism came to Vietnam from the north, by way of China, as did the other major belief systems of the Vietnamese, Confucianism and Taoism. The resultant mix, combined with an indigenous tradition of spirit worship, makes Vietnamese spiritual values both complex and unique.

Mahayana Buddhism is the main religion although ancestor worship is still widely practised. You will find altars in many houses, with offerings and photographs of parents and grandparents. Confucian philosophy has influenced morals, and family ties are strong. Familial loyalty and obedience are central to the Vietnamese social structure. The Taoist idea of balance and harmony has also influenced the way the Vietnamese see the world.

Nearly 10 percent of the population are Catholic, a legacy of French colonial times. Most of them live in the south. There is a substantial Theravada Buddhist minority among the ethnic Khmers of the Mekong Delta, and there are small Muslim communities of South Asian origin in Hanoi and Ho Chi Minh City. The Chams of the central coast are Hindu, while those of the Mekong Delta are Muslim. Indigenous Vietnamese religions include the wildly syncretic Cao Dai, with its centre at Tay Ninh in the south, and the modified Buddhist Hoa Hao, centred on Chau Doc in the Mekong Delta.

T

TELEPHONE, FAX & EMAIL

The country code for Vietnam is 84. The city code for Hanoi is 04, for Ho Chi Minh City 08. Other important area codes are as follows: Dalat 063; Danang and Hoi An 051; Halong 033; Hue 054; Nha Trang 058. The leading 0 is dropped when making an international call to Vietnam. To make an IDD call, dial the international prefix 00, followed by the country code, area code and the number.

International calls can be made from most hotels, where rooms will usually have a telephone, but call charges are very high – some of the most expensive in the world. The hotel will also add on a hefty service charge. Calls can also be made from post offices. Ringing from the post office is cheaper, but you will be charged for the first three minutes whether you use them or not. Reverse charges (collect calls) are not permitted.

Most good hotels and post offices offer an adequate fax service, but again costs are fairly high.

Internet cafés have now sprung up all over Vietnam and emailing is possible from even the smallest town. Costs are very low and this is by far the best way of keeping in contact with friends and family.

I want to make a call to...	**Toi muon goi ...**

TIME DIFFERENCES

Vietnam is 7 hours ahead of Greenwich Mean Time (GMT + 7). The chart below shows the times in Vietnam and various other cities across the world.

New York	London	Johannesburg	**Vietnam**	Sydney	Auckland
Midnight	5am	6am	**Noon**	2pm	4pm

TIPPING

Tipping was never a part of traditional Vietnamese culture, but these days it is appreciated. If you feel you have been well looked after a small token of thanks would not be out of place. Most hotels and top restaurants will add a service charge to your bill. Tipping tour guides, waiters and car drivers is becoming more common.

Is service (tip) included?	**Da tinh tien hau ban vao hoa don chua?**

TOILETS

Most tourist hotels have Western-style toilets, but you may find a few with the more locally common squat toilet. Almost all public toilets and restaurants have squat-style conveniences. It's a good idea to carry your own toilet paper and if there's a waste bin next to the toilet the used paper should be deposited there rather than in the toilet. In many establishments the plumbing is not good enough to handle waste paper.

Where are the toilets, please? **Nha ve sinh o dau?**

TOURIST INFORMATION

Vietnam has yet to develop a network of tourist information offices overseas. For visa and travel information, you should contact the Embassy of the Socialist Republic of Vietnam in your capital:

Australia: 6 Timbarra Crescent, O'Malley, ACT 2606; tel: 2-62866059; fax: 2-62864534; email: <canberra@au.vnembassy.org>; <www.au.vnembassy.org>. Consulate: 489 New South Head Road, Double Bay, Sydney, NSW 2028; tel: 2-93272539; fax: 2-93281653; email: <vnconsul@ihug.com.au>.

Canada: 226 Maclaren Street, Ottawa, ONT K2P OL6; tel: 613-236 0772; fax: 613-236 2704; email: <vietnam@istar.ca>.

South Africa: 87 Brooks Street, Brooklyn PO Box 13692, Hatfield 0028, Pretoria; tel: 12-362 8119; fax: 12-362 8115; email: <em bassy@vietnam.co.za>.

United Kingdom: 12–14 Victoria Road, London W8 5RD; tel: 0871 717 1726; fax: 020 7937 6108.

United States: 1233 20th Street NW, Suite 400, Washington, DC 20036; tel: (202) 861 0737; fax: (202) 861 0917; email: <info@vietnamembassy-usa.org>. Consulate: 1700 Califomia Street, Suite 475, San Francisco, CA 94109; tel: (415) 922 1707; Fax: (415) 922 1848; email: <info@vietnamconsulate-sf.org>.

Within Vietnam, the state-run body that theoretically looks after visitors is Vietnam Tourism, with its head office at 80 Quan Su, Hanoi; tel: (04) 942 1061; email: <vnat@vietnam-tourism.com>. Its network of regional offices throughout the country provide information and services such as transport hire, hotel reservations and various tours. These are the tourist offices in three major cities:
Hanoi: Hanoi Tourism, 18 Ly Thuong Kiet; tel: 826 6714.
Ho Chi Minh City: Saigon Tourist, 49 Le Thanh Ton; tel: 829 8129.
Hue: Hue-Thua Thien Tourism, 15 Le Loi, Hue; tel: 822 369.

Another state organisation, Trung Tam Du Lich Thanh Nien Vietnam (Vietnam's Youth Tourism Centre), is very helpful and can orgise tailor-made tours. Contact them at 31 Cao Thang, District 3, Ho Chi Minh City; tel: 829 0553.

Where is the tourist office?	**Van phong huong dan khach du lich o dau?**

W

WEBSITES

The Vietnam National Administration of Tourism website at <www.vietnamtourism.com> is full of good information on the country and its people, as well as hotel and restaurant tips. For business and general news on the country try <www.vietnamnews.net> and <http://www.vnn.vn/english/>.

Y

YOUTH HOSTELS

There are no organised youth hostels in Vietnam, though cheap dormitory accommodation is available in most cities. Unless you're on a very tight budget indeed, these cannot really be recommended.

Recommended Hotels

Though Vietnam's hotel scene does not quite match up to nearby destinations like Hong Kong and Thailand, it is catching up fast, with growing tourist numbers fuelling a building boom. This is good news for visitors, who can often find a new place with smart rooms at competitive prices. Generally, though not exclusively, the large, state-run hotels are run by indifferent staff, while low and mid-range mini-hotels are often operated by families who will do all they can to make their guests happy. Most places above US$10 include at least a basic breakfast, and top-end places can be very plush, with carpeted floors, air-conditioning, baths, satellite TV and minibar. Many hotels have good websites that can help you make a choice, and Internet bookings often give cheaper rates. Reservations are not generally necessary, except during major festivals such as *Tet*. Prices given below are for a double or twin room during high season, and most places will give considerable discounts during the low season.

$$$ over US$50
$$ US$15–50
$ under US$15

HANOI

Anh Dao $$ *37 Ma May; tel: (04) 826 7151; email: <camellia @hn.vnn.vn>*. Located in the heart of Hanoi's Old Quarter, this budget hotel has well-maintained rooms, some with balconies and baths, and helpful and friendly staff.

Dan Chu $$$ *29 Trang Tien; tel: (04) 825 4937; fax: 826 6786.* There's a nostalgic feel about this old French hotel situated a short way south of Hoan Kiem Lake. Its rooms have attractive wooden fittings and spacious bathrooms. The hotel also has a massage service (about $5 an hour) that is rated the city's best.

Galaxy $$ *1 Phan Dinh Phung; tel: (04) 828 2888; fax: 828 2466.* On the northern fringe of the Old Quarter, this 60-room hotel has comfortable, well-equipped lodgings. Attractive restaurant.

Guoman $$$ *83a Ly Thuong Kiet; tel: (04) 822 2800; fax: 822 2800; email: <guomanhn@hn.vnn.vn>.* A good business hotel near the railway station, with business centre, health club and several restaurants, and prices significantly cheaper than the top hotels.

Hanoi Horison $$$ *40 Cat Linh; tel: (04) 733 0808; fax: 733 0888.* One of the city's more tasteful hotels, located a little west of the centre. Attractively decorated rooms and a good business centre.

Hilton Hanoi Opera $$$ *1 Le Thanh Tong; tel: (04) 933 0500; fax: 933 0530; <www.hilton.com>.* Located beside the Opera House, this dazzling hotel has a fitness centre, pool and nightclub.

Melia Hanoi $$$ *44b Ly Thuong Kiet; tel: (04) 934 3343; fax: 934 3344; email: <solmelia@meliahotel.com>.* Somewhat cheaper than other top hotels like the Hilton and Sofitel Metropole. The building itself is not very attractive, but the luxurious rooms have all conveniences, and there is also a rooftop swimming pool.

Nam Phuong $$ *26 Nha Chung; tel: (04) 824 6894.* A small hotel with light, airy rooms near the Cathedral, an area of Hanoi that is full of character and ideally situated for seeing the major sights.

Queen $ *65 Hang Bac; tel: (04) 826 0860; fax: 826 0300; email: <queenaz@fpt.vn>.* A good budget alternative in the heart of the Old Quarter, offering a variety of clean, compact rooms.

Quoc Hoa $$ *10 Bat Dan; tel: (04) 828 4528; fax: 826 7424; email: <quochoa@hn.vnn.vn>.* Excellent facilities and stylish rooms give this place an upmarket feel, but the prices are very affordable.

Royal $$$ *20 Hang Tre; tel: (04) 824 4230.* A smallish but luxurious hotel to the northeast of Hoan Kiem Lake with tastefully decorated rooms and a convenient location.

Sofitel Metropole $$$ *15 Ngo Quyen; tel: (04) 826 6919.* Hanoi's most lavish hotel, dating back to 1901, exudes a colonial charm that is difficult to beat. It is very popular, not only for its rooms, but also for its pool, its top-quality restaurants and cosy bars.

HO CHI MINH CITY

An An $$ *40 Bui Vien Street; tel: (08) 837 8087, <www.ananhotel.com>*. New mini-hotel in the budget district with 20 bright and airy rooms, all with air-conditioning and baths, and some with computers. $1 buffet breakfast in the 11th-floor restaurant.

Caravelle $$$ *19 Lam Son Square; tel: (08) 823 4999; fax: 824 3999; <www.caravellehotel.com>*. Located just opposite the Municipal Theatre in the heart of the city, this legendary establishment maintains its status as the city's most prestigious hotel. Luxurious rooms and suites, impeccable service and a relaxing rooftop bar.

Continental $$$ *132–4 Dong Khoi; tel: (08) 829 9203; fax: 829 0936; <www.continentalvietnam.com>*. Made famous as a haunt for war journalists, this grand old colonial building has carpeted stairs, marbled floors, plush rooms and a nice café in a restful courtyard.

Four Roses $$ *790–95 Nguyen Dinh Chieu; tel/fax: (08) 832 5895; email: <eroseminne@hcm.vnn.vn>*. Surrounded by a colourful flower garden, this hotel, run by a friendly French-speaking family, has 10 immaculately clean, pleasantly furnished rooms, each with its own balcony. A long way west of the city centre, but exceptional.

Grand $$$ *8 Dong Khoi; tel: (08) 823 0163; fax: 823 5781; <www.grandsaigon.com>*. This lovely old building dates back to the 1930s, and has recently been restored to its original grandeur. Sumptuous furnishings and fittings and highly polished floors give an aura of elegance to this well-positioned hotel on Dong Khoi near the river. Other facilities include swimming pool and massage service.

Hotel 127 $ *127 Cong Quynh; tel: (08) 836 8761; email: <guest house127@bdvn.vnd.net>*. Madam Cuc, the welcoming owner of this small hotel, makes sure that the rooms here are spotless, and keeps her guests happy with free fruit, tea and coffee. Pick-up from the airport can be arranged. A favourite among backpackers.

Hotel 211 $ *211–13 Pham Ngu Lao; tel: (08) 836 7353; email: <hotelduy@hotmail.com>*. One of the cheapest places in the budget district, with over 60 rooms, some air-conditioned, others with fan. Staff hire out bikes and can help with travel arrangements.

Legend $$$ *2a–4a Ton Duc Thang Street; tel: (08) 823 3333/2333; <www.legendhotelsaigon.com>*. Gazing out over Ton Duc Thang and the Saigon River, this huge new hotel appears monolithic from the outside, but once inside the glittering lobby, you are enveloped by luxury. Its 283 rooms are equipped with every possible convenience.

Majestic $$$ *1 Dong Khoi; tel: (08) 829 5517; fax: 829 5510; <www.majestic-saigon.com>*. This riverfront hotel, built in the 1920s, is packed with character. Some rooms have river views and all are very tastefully decorated. Very friendly, helpful staff.

Renaissance Riverside $$$ *8–15 Ton Duc Thang; tel: (08) 822 0033; fax: 823 5666.* This modern hotel, in a great location by the river and with the country's highest atrium and an attractive pool, has already won an award as Best Luxury Hotel in Vietnam. Despite its size, it has the feel of a boutique hotel.

Sofitel Plaza $$$ *17 Le Duan; tel: (08) 824 1555; email: <sofsgn-resa@hcmc.netnam.vn>*. One of the city's most impressive hotels, with luxurious rooms and a rooftop pool. Wonderful lobby.

NHA TRANG

Ana Mandara Resort $$$ *Beachside Tran Phu; tel: (058) 829 829; email: <wresvana@dng.vnn.vn>*. Nha Trang's most luxurious hotel, on a quiet stretch of beach. The attractive villas and suites have all mod cons as well as traditional touches such as ethnic minority tapestries. Two pools, tennis courts, a spa and beach restaurant.

Bao Dai's Villas $$$ *Tran Phu; tel: (058) 590 147; email: <baodai@dng.vnn.vn>.* A few kilometres south of town, this is the former holiday home of the emperor of Vietnam: five villas divided into rooms and suites, and surrounded by well-kept gardens. Some great views out to sea, and a delightful terrace restaurant.

Nha Trang Lodge $$$ *42 Tran Phu; tel: (058) 810 500; email: <nt-lodge@dng.vnn.vn>.* One of Nha Trang's biggest and fanciest hotels, with over 120 rooms in a high-rise tower that dominates the beach. Facilities include disco, business centre and restaurants.

Perfume Grass Inn $$ *4A Biet Thu; tel: (058) 826 345; email: <huanaz@dng.vnn.vn>.* A small hotel with lots of character in the budget district. Some rooms have wood-panelled floors, others have reclining chairs and baths. Attractive, cheap café downstairs.

Vien Dong $$ *1 Tran Hung Dao; tel: (058) 821 606; email: <vien donghtl@dng.vnn.vn>.* One of Nha Trang's oldest, most reliable hotels with a pool, tennis courts, satellite TV, currency exchange and a decent restaurant (often with live music and traditional dance).

Violet $ *12A Biet Thu; tel: (058) 814 314; email: <ctminhhoang @dng.vnn.vn>.* A mini-hotel in the budget district. Good-sized, air-conditioned rooms and smaller fan-cooled rooms; the staff can help you arrange trips and bicycle or motorbike hire.

HUE

Century Riverside $$ *49 Le Loi; tel: (054) 823 390.* Luxurious, grand hotel on the south bank of the Perfume River with comfortable rooms, souvenir shops and a swimming pool.

Huong Giang $$ *51 Le Loi; tel: (054) 822 122.* Stylish hotel, with cosy rooms, pool and top-floor restaurant. Friendly staff.

Thanh Noi $$ *3 Dang Dung; tel: (054) 522 478.* Ideally located in the Citadel, within walking distance of the Imperial City, this place has characterful, budget rooms and a small pool.

HOI AN

Cua Dai $$ *18a Cua Dai; tel: (0510) 862 231.* Of all the beautiful old colonial buildings in Hoi An, this is one of the finest. It is situated a short walk from the town centre, with a small number of delightfully furnished rooms, many with balconies. Helpful staff.

Hoi An $$ *6 Tran Hung Dao; tel: (0510) 861 373.* This is a large, government-run hotel with over 100 rooms, covering a wide range from small and simple with fan up to large suites with fridge, telephone and air-conditioning. A reasonable pool.

Victoria Hoi An Resort $$$ *Cua Dai Beach; tel: (0510) 927 040; <www.victoriahotels-asia.com>.* Lying just 5km (3 miles) east of the town centre, this hotel has a fabulous private beach frontage and gorgeous rooms, with extra options, such as a pool and spa.

DALAT

Dreams $ *151 Phan Dinh Phung; tel: (063) 833 748; email: <dreams@hcm.vnn.vn>.* Very clean, family-run, mini-hotel just north of the town centre. The rooms are well-equipped and have modern bathrooms. Generous free breakfasts.

Lyla $$ *5 Nam Ky Khoi Nghia; tel: (063) 820 051; email: <lylahotel@hcm.vnn.vn>.* Family-run mini-hotel, set above the lake. Smartly furnished rooms, some with good views. Lovely restaurant.

Sofitel Dalat Palace $$$ *12 Tran Phu; tel: (063) 825 444; email: <sofitel@bdvn.vnd.net>.* Extensive renovations have restored this magnificent colonial-style hotel to its 1930s splendour. All rooms have fantastic views and are lavishly equipped. Drinks are served on the garden terrace, and there's a rooftop bar.

Villa Hotel 28 $$ *28 Tran Hung Dao; tel: (063) 822 764.* This hotel on the southeastern fringe of town has the feel of an English country home. It consists of one main building, with nice garden views, and a more modern annexe. Guests have access to a cosy sitting room.

Recommended Restaurants

Sampling some of the regional cuisine in Vietnam would be enough reason to visit the country in itself, and the locals' sense of style means there are some truly memorable environments in which to enjoy the subtlety and variety of Vietnamese food. Most of the hotels listed on the previous pages have good restaurants, but those recommended below are more personal places, many of them with tasteful decor, delicious food and often an intimate atmosphere too. Prices given are for an average main dish for one person, and those restaurants with phone numbers are so popular that it's better to call ahead and reserve a table.

$$$	over US$10
$$	US$3–10
$	under US$3

HANOI

Brother's Café $$$ *26 Nguyen Thai Hoc; tel: (04) 733 3866.* A stylishly-restored temple is the exotic location for set Vietnamese dinners and lunches: meditate on your food or the peaceful surroundings.

Cyclo $$ *38 Duong Thanh.* Eat surrounded by cyclos at this smart place that fuses French and Vietnamese cuisine in surprising ways. Choose between the air-conditioned dining room and the quiet, shady rear garden. The set lunches for less than $5 are a bargain.

Emperor $$ *18b Le Thanh Tong.* Here you can combine eating tasty Vietnamese food with entertainment. A choice of indoor or outdoor eating, and traditional music played on Wednesday and Saturday evenings, while Tuesdays and Fridays a Latin band performs.

Gecko $$$ *14b Bao Khanh.* A mouthwatering menu of appetisers and main courses such as sautéed shrimp Provençale tossed with fettuccine. Chef Michel Seyve creates some of the most original and delicious sauces you are likely to taste anywhere.

Hoa Sua $$ *28a Ha Hoi; tel: (04) 942 4448.* A remarkable establishment which trains disadvantaged children for careers in catering, and does so with resounding success. Vietnamese food with a strong French influence; garden patio and a bright dining room.

Indochine $$$ *16 Nam Ngu; tel: (04) 942 4097.* Fantastic ambience and food make this a hit with expats. Eat inside the cosy colonial house or in the courtyard. House specialities include prawns on sugar cane or chicken and banana flower salad.

Luna d'Autonno $$ *11b Dien Bien Phu; tel: (04) 823 7338.* Serves some of the best pizzas in Hanoi, and has a delivery service too. Breakfast available in the snack bar downstairs and dinner served in the dining room upstairs. Hosts jazz events at weekends.

Nam Phuong $$$ *19 Phan Chu Trinh; tel: (04) 824 0926.* Elegant atmosphere in and around an imposing colonial villa, with a good range of traditional Vietnamese dishes, but prices are rather steep. The walls are enlivened with paintings by local artist Pham Luan.

No Noodles $ *20 Nha Chung.* When you can't face another bowl of rice or noodles, head on down to No Noodles and order up a sandwich of your own design, served up in a crunchy baguette.

Three Mountains $$ *34 Ba Trieu.* A stylishly-renovated colonial villa with intriguing paintings on the wall and occasional piano/violin duets to entertain customers. Relaxing atmosphere, traditional Vietnamese food superbly prepared, and service second-to-none.

HO CHI MINH CITY

Blue Ginger $$ *37 Nam Ky Khoi Nghia.* The refined, low-ceilinged dining room has eye-catching artwork on the walls, traditional live evening music and top-quality Vietnamese dishes. Agreeable ambience and great food.

Camargue $$$ *16 Cao Ba Quat.* An expensive French restaurant set in colonial-style modern villa, surrounded by a leafy courtyard. Comfortable chairs and old wooden ceiling fans create the feel of a bygone era. Gourmet food and a good range of wines.

Chao Thai $$ *16 Thai Van Lung; tel: (08) 824 1457.* This small restaurant is lavishly decorated with Thai-style motifs and serves the best Thai food in town. Try the *yam tua plu* (winged bean salad) or the *hor mok talay* (seafood curry in banana leaves).

Lemongrass $$ *4 Nguyen Thiep.* A traditional upmarket establishment serving good Vietnamese food beautifully presented. While customers eat they are serenaded by traditional musicians.

Manderine $$$ *11a Ngo Van Nam; tel: (08) 822 9783.* This long-established upmarket restaurant, with beautiful traditional decor, serves well-prepared Vietnamese standards. Fairly expensive: the set menus offer the best value. Live traditional music in evenings.

Ngoc Suong Marina $$ *19c Le Qui Don.* This is the newest branch of one of the most popular seafood restaurants in town, drawing big crowds every evening. Try the hot and sour fish soup or the steamed fish in beer.

Ngon $ *138 Nam Ky Khoi Nghia; tel: (08) 825 7179.* One of the best culinary experiences in the city, at rock-bottom prices. Delicious regional specialities are served in and around a delightful colonial building. It's very popular, so book or be ready to queue.

Qucina $$$ *7 Cong Truong; tel: (08) 824 6325.* An Italian restaurant beneath the Municipal Theatre and next to Q Bar, one of the trendiest bars in town and under the same ownership. It has minimalist decor and some of the best pizzas and pasta in town.

Underground $$ *basement of Lucky Plaza, 69 Dong Khoi.* This basement place draws in an eclectic crowd of foreigners to sample its great Western food served in generous portions. Try the succulent New Zealand grilled steaks, which are as thick as your fist.

Vietnam House $$ *93–95 Dong Khoi.* Situated in a delightful, shuttered colonial building, an excellent place to try traditional Vietnamese food. It features staff in traditional outfits, a pianist on the ground floor and traditional folk music upstairs.

NHA TRANG

Cyclo Café $ *5a Tran Quang Khai.* This small restaurant has delightful decor, friendly ambience, and an extensive menu of well-priced Vietnamese, Italian and vegetarian food.

La Bella Napoli $$ *Tran Phu.* Situated on the beachfront just north of the Thuy Duong, La Bella Napoli produces some of the city's best home-made pizza and pasta, as well as Italian-style seafood. Good coffee and ice creams too.

Ngoc Suong $$ *16 Tran Quang Khai.* This smart seafood restaurant, tucked away near the budget district, offers a fantastic range of seafood dishes, priced according to weight.

Same Same But Different $ *111b Nguyen Thien Thuat.* This is the place to head for when you dream of a good bowl of muesli or plate of hash browns, though they also serve a wide range of Vietnamese and other Western dishes at very reasonable prices.

Thuy Duong $$ *junction of Le Thanh Ton and Tran Phu.* Located on the beachfront, with candle-lit terraces, tasteful surroundings and fresh seafood that you can choose from the aquarium tank.

Truc Linh $$ *21 Biet Thu.* A smart restaurant with a wide-ranging menu that includes a choice of Vietnamese and Western food and a mouth-watering seafood selection at very competitive prices.

HUE

Dong Tam $$ *48 Le Loi.* A good spot for a vegetarian lunch in the garden courtyard of a Buddhist family home. The menu is rather limited but prices are cheap and the set menus are good value.

Ngu Ha $$ *181 Xuan 68; tel: (054) 513 320.* An ancient Hue house is the setting for refined eating of traditional royal food, with Hue music too.

Song Huong Floating Restaurant $$ *Le Loi Street, tel: 826 655.* Though the Vietnamese food in this restaurant on the river is quite reasonable, the location is the main attraction: enjoy a sun-downer here at the end of the day.

HOI AN

Café des Amis $$ *52 Bach Dang.* When you just can't decide what you want to eat, this is the place to go. There's no menu, but the French-speaking owner, Mr Kim, turns out a fantastic four-course vegetarian meal that never fails to surprise and delight.

Mermaid $$ *2 Tran Phu.* This cosy little restaurant has a wide menu of Vietnamese and Western dishes, but is especially popular for its three-course set dinners at extremely good prices.

Miss Ly $ *22 Nguyen Hue.* This place is famous for two local dishes – *cao lau* and *banh bao* – a delicious noodle soup with beansprouts and small parcels of crab and shrimp meat.

DALAT

Long Hoa $$ *6, 3 Thang 2.* An intimate, family-run restaurant in the heart of town, serving up great Vietnamese dishes and reasonable steaks as well. Delicious strawberry wine and home-made yoghurt too.

Trong Dong $$ *220 Phan Dinh Phung.* Small but smart Vietnamese restaurant with a good range of well-priced dishes and attentive service. Try the Vietnamese special salad, which includes shrimps, peanuts, pork and herbs.

V Cafe $ *1/1 Bui Thi Xuan.* A smart but cosy café that has a surprisingly varied menu of Vietnamese and Western dishes, including burgers, tacos and soups. The home-made cakes are also excellent.

INDEX